equipped2succeed

'Create your own future history'.
Muhammed Ali

Empowered – Enabled – Equipped

Beverley Burton

Published by

equipped2succeed
Nottingham UK

Version 1.0

First published in 2018

ISBN 978-0-9926678-4-9

This book is dedicated to all those who have helped me – who have supported my journey and from whom I have learned and continue to learn.

A special thank you to my father who passed in 2016: I miss the open, honest sharing of ideas . . . without judgment. Thank you for your insights and wisdom.

Above all, thank you to my children: Harriet and George, who have grown up with the development of equipped2succeed. I look at you in awe and wonder every day and always value your honest, frank feedback and unconditional support.

Contents

Preface

There are thousands of self-development books out there so why should you read this one? I don't kid myself that I have anything that is completely new or original to say. My focus has been putting something together that thinks about our development as whole people living whole lives. Compartmentalising our lives may be thought of as a necessity, but the reality is that most of us move seamlessly between all the things in our lives, and our working lives have become far less 9-5. The same understanding and skills we need in professional relationships, for example, are the same ones we need in personal relationships with friends, family and children.

There are many books out there that go into depth on the areas covered in this book and you can follow up with those as appropriate. I wanted to give people an overview so they could look holistically, acknowledge areas where they're already brilliant and decide where they need to focus their development next. I wanted this book to enable people to: self-reflect, realise, acknowledge and celebrate what they do well, and share insights and tools that help people to be even more brilliant in areas they need to improve to reach their goals.

Whereas many people do workshops and talks focused on their books, I have definitely done this the other way around, delivering years of education, training and development programmes before writing this book. Working with people face-to-face, facilitating learning in a workshop where you can 'tune-in' with people, discuss, debate and notice body language is very different to writing. However, a book has one huge advantage: you can dip in and out for what you need at the time, go over things to overcome a barrier, reinforce your belief and re-focus where and when you need.

I have attempted to get into this book the underpinning 'stuff' from my workshops and training programmes that have helped people to positively move forward. I hope you enjoy reading *equipped2succeed* and it informs your journey.

Introduction

equipped2succeed

self-determination: *the process by which a person controls their own life.**

It's OK to be exactly who you are because each one of those steps that are happening to you in your life, no matter how peculiar they seem at the time, are terrific because they're preparing you for exactly who you're meant to be.
Sharon Stone

What is different about those who determine their own future? What is different about those who develop and maintain holistic wellbeing? What is different about those who are so obviously comfortable in their own skin? What is different about people who set their own success criteria and reach their goals? What is different about individuals who make a real, positive difference in their community, in the world, in their field, in others' lives?

Knowledge and skills are not enough. It doesn't matter where people start, socially, educationally or economically, (or what hurdles they face en route), those who succeed in achieving the happiness, success and wellbeing that we all seek share similar thinking, attitudes and behaviours. They do not allow external or internal limitations to stop them.

equipped2succeed is about developing what we need to create the future we choose.

* Definitions in this book are derived from the Oxford English Dictionary equipped2succeed is about how we can realise our dreams and potential: overcome internal and external limitations and succeed in our chosen path for the benefit of ourselves, and those around us.

It is based on my equipped2succeed framework of thinking, attitudes and behaviours which I have come to realise are essential to pursue the life we choose. There are some people to whom these capabilities appear to come more naturally – they are driven and find ways to create the life they choose, despite circumstances, environment and setbacks. However, when we dig, we find that they have largely developed these characteristics through learning from life, learning from experience – their own and others' experience, learning from success and learning from failure. And what's great is that we can learn from them!

I hope that equipped2succeed shares usable and helpful insights and tools that help you reflect and develop in all areas of life. I also hope that it enables you to find your way through, over and round actual and perceived limitations, to be where you're meant to be.

> *The one unchangeable certainty is*
> *that nothing is unchangeable or certain.*
> John F. Kennedy

Our world is uncertain, and constant economic, social, technological and environmental changes mean we all need core capabilities to embrace change and challenge, and make the most of opportunities. Old certainties are going and 'jobs for life' have been replaced by more and more portfolio, self-employed careers. More than ever, we need to be agile in our thinking and prepared to learn, unlearn and relearn as the need arises. We need to be equipped to make the most of ever changing, fast paced environments and balance personal, caring and professional demands. Sometimes we also need to feel more fulfilled – feel we're where we're meant to be rather than on a path we didn't positively choose.

BEING BRAVE (and doing the work!)

> We can overcome the paralysis of fear of change and fear of failure
> by taking action and maintaining forward momentum.

A man who acquires the ability to take full
possession of his own mind
may take possession of anything else to which
he is justly entitled.
Dale Carnegie

90% of success in anything is positively harnessing and using the power of our minds, believing in ourselves and being brave. It also means doing the work, success doesn't just happen, and waiting to get lucky just doesn't work. I firmly believe that;

to succeed we must decide what we want,
decide what we're prepared to pay, in time, energy and effort,
have a growth mindset and go to work.

Many people think successful people are just lucky, just more talented, more driven or have special gifts etc. It is true that successful people have something special, but it's not luck, it's deciding what they want, focusing, being creative, bravely taking opportunities and being prepared to do the work. We obviously need to develop the specific knowledge and skills required in our fields of endeavour, but the essential, core characteristics of successful people are the same in any environment: in fields as diverse as the arts, science, business, academia, engineering, sports, technology and in the media.

Opportunity is missed by most people because it is
dressed in overalls and looks like work.
Thomas Edison

Individuals who have reached that feeling of being where they're meant to be demonstrate the characteristics described in this book, whether that's in maintaining their health and fitness or pursuing work they love. Many develop these qualities by 'osmosis': learning from what's around them, learning the lessons from negative and positive experiences, and from other people. They also demonstrate that these characteristics can be developed. All it takes is the will to learn, grow and improve, the confidence to honestly self-reflect, and the discipline to continuously take action.

Leave Excuses Behind

No more finding yourself saying; *'That's just the way I am.'*
Having a growth mindset is essential to realising our dreams. To grow and improve we need to believe that we can change. This requires accurate, positive self-reflection; not being too critical, or having an inflated view of ourselves. Too many people accept *'That's just the way I am'.* **We all have personality traits, but much of the way we are is learned and can be unlearned. We can all change. We can all achieve more with the right willingness, awareness, knowledge and tools.**

Defining Our Own Version of Success

What does success mean to you? This subject is explored in detail in Chapter Two; *What is Success?* but in general terms, it is about achieving personal, social and economic wellbeing and helping those around us to achieve theirs too. We all seek to make the most of life, and that comes from feeling we're living the positive life we're meant to lead.

Success is NOT what you think it is.
It is what you believe it is . . . and most never believe.
Doug Firebaugh

The journey of creating and delivering the equipped2succeed programmes and materials has reinforced my belief that it is within us all to choose our own future if we are equipped to do so and believe we can. We all make mistakes; the important thing is to learn from them and move on:

Aim for success, not perfection.
Never give up your right to be wrong,
because then you will lose the ability to learn new things
and move forward with your life.
Remember that fear always lurks behind perfectionism.
Confronting your fears and allowing yourself the right to be
human can make you a far happier
and more productive person.
Dr. David M. Burns

Chapter One

Some Essential 'Stuff'

'Stuff': hard to define yet our lives are full of it; it describes everything from challenges we face to the 'good stuff'; which is different for us all. In this chapter it's meaning is the 'stuff of life': the fundamental core of things.

So, what do I mean by 'essential stuff'?

In order to equip ourselves to succeed there are a few things that underpin our development. Let me start with some definitions of attitude, thinking and behavior.

Attitude: *A feeling or opinion about something or someone, or a way of behaving that is caused by this;*
A settled way of thinking or feeling, typically reflected in a person's behaviour.
A state of mind or a feeling;
A position of the body or manner of carrying oneself; implying an action or mental state.

I am the only person who can control my attitude in any given circumstance. As my attitude has enormous influence over my thinking, responses, behaviour and performance, it's crucial that I choose my attitude to achieve positive outcomes.

Thinking: *The act or practice of one who thinks; thought.*
A way of reasoning: judgement: characterised by thought or thoughtfulness;
When you use your mind to consider something;
Someone's ideas or opinions.

Behaviour: *The way that someone behaves - the manner of behaving or conducting oneself.*
Actions and reactions in different circumstances.

In terms of developing our attitudes, thinking and behaviours there are a few things I view as part of our foundation or bedrock.

Development - Accurate Self-reflection

Your commitment to **C**onstant **A**nd **N**ever-ending **I**mprovement (**C.A.N.I.**) is obvious, given that you are reading this book. Let's acknowledge and accept a few things that underpin development:

- there's not one way to develop;
- there are many ways to learn and you need to find the right blend for you in any given area of development such as: reading, coaching, mentoring, training and finding the right way to expand your comfort zone;
- we all have strengths and things we need to improve;
- accurate, positive, critical self-reflection is essential;
- seek and use the views and reflections of those around you. NB – *use the reflections of those around you that help you grow and develop* and *ditch the ones that place limitations on you or your thinking.*

What's important is to challenge ourselves in areas that are vital to improving our personal and professional lives.

Values

Values are like fingerprints. Nobody's are the same, but you leave 'em all over everything you do.
Elvis Presley

Values are the ideals, customs and institutions for which we have an effective regard. These values may be positive such as cleanliness, freedom, or education, or negative such as cruelty or crime.

Values are important because they are the foundation upon which we make important decisions in our lives: with whom we are friends, how we treat people, and how we view the world.

Our attitudes, thinking and behaviours, our aspirations and expectations, are all shaped in some way or other by our values. They are established and develop as we grow, and those we are closest to in our early lives have a major impact on them.

They are the things that are important to us, the essence of what we believe in: *love, calmness, faith, personal growth, making a difference, courage, honesty, confidence, financial security, financial independence, self-determination, friendship, making a contribution, determination, integrity, respect for others' heritage, culture and individuality, caring* – the list goes on.

We all need to decide what values are most important for us. For most of us, this is not something we consciously decide and write down, but rather an unwritten set of values that emerges and develops as we grow. Sometimes we accept the values we develop as children and young people and sometimes we need to re-assess. Our values underpin every decision we make and are therefore worth spending some time reflecting on.

The following questions are a starting point for you to define or re-define your values:

- What do you believe in? God and islam which encourage me to respect the people who maybe treat me badly..
- What are the qualities you think are important in people? honest and faith
- What are the qualities you want to develop in yourself to be the person you want to be? Strong courage and believe in myself more (trust my senses)
- What are the things you think it's important to achieve for yourself and for others? The dreams

- What things are most important to you?
1- To do my best and be happy with it
2- don't carry ever and never about the people who upset me (and say that I can't)
3- don't trust people
4- Try to balance bettewen my brain and my heart in any suttiation

13

Do What You Say You're Going To Do, When You Say You're Going To Do It!

We all know how vital this is in relationships with family, friends, partners, colleagues and customers. There are always times we need to change plans, and that's a part of life. It's important to remember that people view us by how we behave 40% of the time, as if we behave like that all the time. The bottom line is that we need to do what we say we're going to do when we say we're going to do it *most* of the time!

Accept that We are Human and We Get Things Wrong

It's important to acknowledge when we fail (without beating ourselves up about it), apologise and move on. That takes courage and confidence. Some people wrongly see apologising as a weakness. On the contrary, it shows tremendous strength to say sorry (as long as it's not a constant self-depreciating response), and people appreciate it so much as they are generally unused to individuals or organisations admitting their mistakes and apologising. Being prepared to admit when you're wrong and authentically apologise, without shame, is very valuable in building and maintaining good relationships. However, it's vital that we don't let getting things wrong undermine our confidence and self-regard. We can embrace it as a learning opportunity.

In addition, there is a world of difference between being constantly apologetic, which indicates low self-regard, and or thinking that, as long as we apologise it's OK to keep messing up. I mean a genuine apology: having the confidence to acknowledge, apologise and move on when we make a mistake, and doing everything we can not to make that same mistake again.

Getting things wrong once or twice is forgivable. Repeatedly getting the same things wrong makes our apologies worthless.

'I'm just like that' is usually an excuse for inappropriate, unhelpful behaviours and habits that we choose not to do anything about.

professional circumstances. It also includes feeling valued and valuing others. What are your success criteria when it comes to relationships?

Education / Learning / Development
I am fortunate that I have always loved learning, and my growth mindset is ever-present; on too many fronts at once sometimes! Having a growth mindset and learning in all sorts of ways is essential to develop, personally and professionally. Where are you now in your learning and development? Are there key capabilities you need to work on? Are there skills, courses, study or training that you want to, or need to, focus on to achieve your goals?

Career / Business
Economic, personal and family wellbeing often come together in a career, business or endeavour which brings the personal rewards that contribute to our happiness and wellbeing, and the financial rewards that enable us to support our family. What are your career / business success criteria?

Pursuing Interests
We all have things that are important to us; that we enjoy for their own sake or as part of our personal ambition. These can develop and change with age and experience. I didn't like writing when I was younger, as I didn't think I was any good at it - my spelling was poor and it took me a long time to translate my thinking into writing. I was a doer! Finding my passion and pursuing it, has however, lead to me to enjoy writing. Does this come in the interest or career section? With me, it's definitely both. What do you love to do? How could you do more of what you love to do?

For those who succeed in their field of endeavor there is usually a cross-over from their interests to the way they earn a living, and their personal passions turn into career or business interests. As Richard Branson says,

I don't really separate work and play – it's all living.
This doesn't mean I'm always working,
it means I've learned the art of balance.

We could no doubt debate *What is Success?* for hours, and I have done with lots of people, but the bottom line is that we need to decide what success means for us as individuals.

Once you know what you want to achieve:

> **The will to win, the desire to succeed, the urge to reach your full potential... these are the keys that will unlock the door to personal excellence.**
> Confucious

How do we measure success? There are different measurements in different contexts. The wheel of life helps us to graphically see which aspects we're happy with and which to focus on.

equipped2succeed Wheel of Life

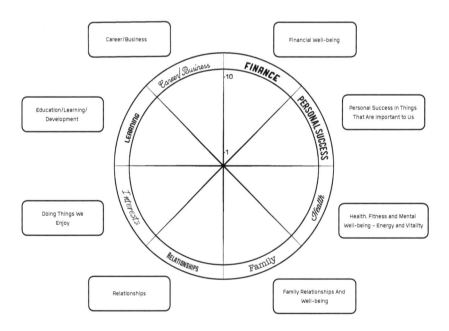

Choosing and accepting the consequences of that choice are crucial aspects of feeling empowered because it involves being able to control what happens to us, and being in control of our life. Part of this is accepting responsibility for our mistakes. Making mistakes and learning from them, rather than being floored by them, is vital if we are to succeed. Taking responsibility brings about positive results and enables us to achieve our goals.

Life is not the way it's supposed to be. It's the way it is.
The way you cope with it is what makes the difference.
Virginia Satir

It's also important to be clear about what is your responsibility and what isn't. It's always a balance and judgment and we can constantly improve with experience and reflection. Abdicating responsibility where we need to be responsible benefits no one. If we take responsibility for things that are someone else's responsibility (when we don't need to) we can disempower them, and it gives us less time and energy to focus on our unique role and goals. We need to take responsibility for things that could make a real positive difference for ourselves, those around us and our purpose.

The main thing is to keep the main thing the main thing.
Stephen Covey

Responsibility rather than excuses

Let us not seek to fix blame for the past; let us accept
responsibility for the future.
John F. Kennedy

Taking responsibility is all about realising that we have the power of self-determination, but we have to grasp it: focus our energies on what's going to take us forward and avoid wasting energy on making excuses or blaming others.

To the question of your life, you are the only answer.
To the problems of your life, you are the only solution.
Jo Coudert

Taking responsibility

Taking responsibility includes believing that in ourselves and believing we are capable. It's worth explicitly reminding ourselves of the following, especially when faced by challenging situations:

I am capable.

I contribute in meaningful ways and I am genuinely needed.

I choose my response to what happens to me.

My feelings are important, and I trust myself to learn from my mistakes. I have self-control and self-discipline.

I know how to speak out, listen, co-operate, share and negotiate for what I want.

I can be counted on, and I tell the truth. Things don't always go my way, but I can adapt when I need to.

I try to solve my own problems, but I know that if I need help, I'll ask for it.

Becoming self-determining individuals (and knowing and feeling that we are) is a vital ingredient for holistic success. The bottom line is that we can only take responsibility for ourselves – our thoughts and behaviour. Self-reliant and self-determining individuals:

- control the controllable;
- ask for help when needed;
- take responsibility for their reaction to events;
- take responsibility for their role in relationships.

Taking Responsibility example Affirmations*

- *I am taking responsibility for creating my own positive future.*
- *I am relishing being responsible for my thoughts, actions and future.*
- *I am responsible for what I think, say and do.*
- *I am responsible for making a contribution.*

*Affirmations are personal positive statements in the first person, present tense that reinforce what we want to be, do and have, as if we've already achieved it. More information on creating affirmations at the equipped2succeed website.

> ***Don't sit down and wait for the opportunities to come;***
> ***you have to get up and make them.***
> Madame C. J. Walker

 ACTION

On You Tube, there's an interesting interview with Will Smith, in which he talks about the importance of understanding that rights and responsibilities are two sides of the same coin and how important it was to him to be taught, at a young age, to take responsibility for himself. It's called *Will Smith, The Secret of Success*. It's well worth watching.

Consciously taking responsibility for our actions and thoughts is challenging. Although often we can allow others to influence or even control our thinking, ultimately no-one has control over what you think but you!

Reflection:

- Decide on one or two areas where you could take more responsibility with your family, at work or in your community. For example; take on a project and see it through to completion or share more of the responsibility for caring for your family. The more we do, the more we can do, and the better we get.

- Define what taking responsibility means to you. When you take responsibility think about:
  - How does taking responsibility make you feel?
  - How do others react when you take responsibility?

- Practice distinguishing between yours and others' responsibilities: as distinct from abdicating responsibility or refusing to go the extra mile to help.

- Think of the most responsible people you know. What are the behaviours that show those people are responsible? What sort of things can you do to model what those who take responsibility do?

- Eliminate any 'excuse culture' and blaming others for things for which you are responsible. Focus on taking responsibility for the outcomes of what you do: both positive and negative. That could simply be reinforcing and celebrating successes, or saying sorry for something you've done (to others or yourself), and saying what you're going to do to prevent that happening again.

  It's essential that we eliminate a 'blame culture' don't make ourselves, or others, feel bad when we get something wrong, but rather take responsibility, see it as a learning opportunity, and move on.

- Use some form of reflective diary so you can step back and reflect on progress.

Hold yourself responsible for a higher standard than anyone else expects of you.
Henry Ward Beecher

I am creating my own positive future.

Chapter Six

Use Your Amazing Winning Brain

Thinking to succeed and thrive.

> *Limitations live only in our minds. But if we use our imaginations, our possibilities become limitless.*
> Jamie Paolinetti

use: *to bring out the capabilities or possibilities of; bring to a more advanced or effective state – use your brain as a means of achieving or accomplishing something;*
amazing: *causing wonder*
winning: *the act of a person who wins;*
brain: *the organ inside the head that controls and co-ordinates mental and physical actions; thought, memory, feelings, and activity.*

We can use the power of our mind to achieve what we want in life or allow our thinking to limit us. That applies equally to realising our educational potential, developing fulfilling personal relationships, reaching the pinnacle of our chosen career or business path or making a positive difference in our community and society.

We've all heard the phrase 'use your brain' or 'use your head'. What do we mean by that and how do we do it? We all think differently, and in-order for us to make the most of our amazing brainpower it helps to understand a little about how our brains work. Developing the ability to effectively manage our thinking is essential to learning, wellbeing and success. It is said that most of us consistently use less than 10% of our brainpower.

Imagine the difference it would make if you marginally increased your ability to use your mind more effectively?

Underpinned by science and research, this chapter is designed to help us to use our mind more effectively and develop the other 11 characteristics in the equipped2succeed framework. It is an overview of the more detailed look at using our brains in my book: *Use Your Amazing Winning Brain*.

> **It's often said that you get out what you put in.**
> **In nothing, has this more truth than with your mind.**

Successful individuals effectively manage their thinking, and are able to choose appropriate thinking, attitudes and behaviours – especially when it matters most. In situations where we can feel under pressure, people who can manage their thinking perform better. Those who achieve wellbeing and success positively use the power of their mind and manage their thinking. They relax, visualise and mentally rehearse, stay calm and focused to perform at their best when it matters most:

- in examinations
- in interviews
- reaching goals
- speaking in public
- learning new things
- pitching new ideas and concepts
- winning in sports
- thriving in a challenging environment
- solving a scientific or engineering challenge
- finding a business solution
- managing their mood
- managing family challenges
- responding to a community challenge
- sailing around the world

Whatever we want to achieve, using the power of our mind more effectively helps our performance.

Those who innovate, survive, create and achieve use the power of their mind to find creative solutions. They can see things in different ways, making important connections across experiences, concepts and ideas. This chapter is about taking control of our thinking and developing our thinking for wellbeing and success.

Those who take control of their future and reach their goals have a growth mindset, expanding their mind and thinking and seeking continuous improvement. Mindset is a simple idea identified by world-renowned Stanford University psychologist Carol Dweck in decades of research on achievement and success. A growth mindset fuels our motivation and productivity to realise our goals.

Limitations live only in our minds. But if we use our imaginations, our possibilities become limitless.
Jamie Paolinetti

Our brain controls our body, all our physical processes, and everything we physically do – from growing our hair to breathing, from walking to dancing, from cooking to kicking a ball. Our mind holds all our experiences and the sum total of what we've learned. Our thoughts grow in our mind where we hold all our beliefs. These determine our confidence, our self-belief, how we can conquer our fears, how persistent we are, and how we respond to situations. We can use our brain power to realise our dreams.

Change your thoughts and you change your world.
Norman Vincent Peale

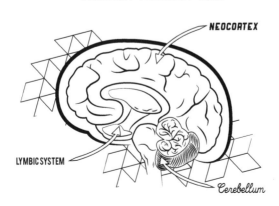

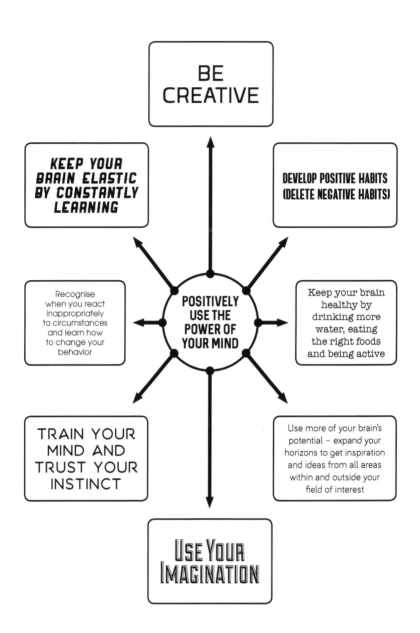

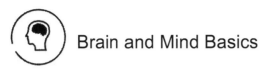

Brain and Mind Basics

A person is what they think about all day long.

The brain takes in all information relating to the body's external and internal environments and produces the appropriate responses. It is composed of several parts that process what we think; how we feel; where we move; what we see, hear, and taste; and all other bodily functions. Taking a brief look at some of the main sections and functions of the brain helps us understand how we can use it more effectively.

Neocortex

The neocortex is the largest portion of the brain and is what distinguishes us from all other mammals.

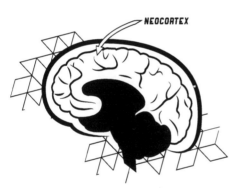

This is our individual, unique 'thinking cap' (yes, that same thinking cap we were told to put on when we were at school!). Knowing something about the power of the neocortex gives us an insight into the infinite possibilities we have within us.

The brain has 80 -100 billion neurons, and the majority of these are in the neocortex. Most of the neurons in the neocortex have between 1,000 and 10,000 synaptic connections with other neurons, enabling the most complex mental activity that we associate with being human.

All that power means we can rewire!

The Limbic System

The limbic system is called the gateway to the cerebral cortex, as most sensory inputs pass through it to the higher levels of the brain. In simple terms, part of its function is to take in information from our senses and decide whether to send the messages to the neocortex or the cerebellum: like a call centre, controlling where information goes next. At the centre of the limbic system is the amygdala. It is known as the emotional centre of the brain (as it plays a key role in the processing of emotions). It impacts how the brain creates emotional memories and responses.

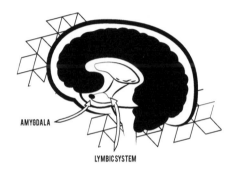

AMYGDALA

LYMBIC SYSTEM

The limbic system is small but extremely powerful. It controls emotions, long-term memory, and determines sleeping and eating patterns.

So, we take in our external environment through the emotional seat of the brain!

Cerebellum

The cerebellum, in evolutionary terms, is the oldest part of the brain. It is sometimes referred to as our 'survival brain', as when our brain perceives we're under threat, the cerebellum moves into automatic survival mode to protect us.

When we're in real or perceived danger, anxious or frightened, we automatically go into our survival mode: Fight, Flight, Flock or Freeze. More on this later.

Cerebellum

Our 'survival brain' also controls balance, co-ordinates movement and maintains muscle tone.

Our Powerhouse of Neurons

Neurons are specialized brain cells that process information. Messages are sent out along the branches of the neuron, called dendrites. These messages are sent out electrically and chemically, forming networks and pathways. All the divisions of the nervous system are based on the functions of neurons. Our nervous systems have four basic types of functional cells:

Sensory neurons: tell the rest of the brain about our external and internal environment. Sensory neurons are activated by information from our senses such as visible light, sound, heat, physical contact or chemical signals, for example in the case of smell or taste.

Motor (and other output) neurons: carry signals from the spinal cord to the muscles to produce movement, and other output neurons stimulate glands and organs.

Communication neurons: transmit signals from one brain area to another.

Computation neurons: The vast majority of our neurons are computation neurons. Computation neurons **extract and process information coming in from the senses, compare that information to what's in our memory, and use the information to plan and execute behavior.**

Developing the connections between these neurons enables us to learn physical skills, knowledge, attitudes and behaviours. How to walk, talk, ride a bike, play a game, learn dance steps, learn processes, solve puzzles, learn language, solve scientific problems, cook, plan, relate to others, develop socially acceptable behaviour, overcome fears: everything. **Developing or 're-wiring' our neural pathways also enables us to move our thinking to the next level, just as you move to the next level in computer games by practising, trying new things and learning, gaining new insights to perform better and achieve our goals.**

Right and Left Brain

Although there is on-going debate amongst neuroscientists, the left side of the brain is said to be the seat of language and processes in a logical and sequential order. The right side is more visual and processes intuitively, holistically and randomly. However, brain research confirms that **neurons from both sides of the brain are involved in most human activity.** It's therefore important for us to develop both 'sides' to improve our thinking.

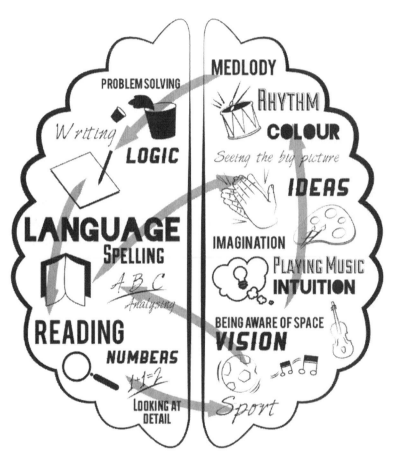

We are at our best when we use the collective power of our brain to best effect. As we learn things, such as your first chord on the guitar, our brain makes up a series of connections or neural pathways. This involves melody, rhythm and spatial awareness, but it also involves reading, sequence and detail.

We see this development of neural pathways using both sides of our brains in all human endeavour from business to sports. If the creative Managing Director, who also manages people well, is absent the Finance Director, who has a grasp of the numbers but poor people skills, is limited in what they can achieve. If the Operations Director isn't there, the creative Managing Director is out of their depth trying to manage systems and processes. They need each other. Leaders of small businesses need to be especially self-aware, and realise where they need specialist help to balance and counter balance their strengths. The greatest, most creative, footballers demonstrate using both sides of their brain all the time, seeing the big picture on the field, analysing, seeing that perfect pass and then accurately passing the ball. The best players use the power of their mind; visualising and mentally rehearsing scoring a goal, celebrating a goal or lifting a trophy.

> *Every goal I ever scored was with my head.*
> Thierry Henry

To achieve our goals and maintain our wellbeing we use both sides of our brain. Being 'in flow' allows our mind to tap into our immense brain power to solve problems, come up with solutions, and find ways to do things better.

All our learning and behaviour is affected by our emotional state.

Our brain performs best when we are 'in flow'; relaxed and focused. This allows our brain to make the right connections between neurons, between the right and left sides of our brain. If we are stressed or anxious, we don't perform at our best, whether that's learning something new, in examinations, in sport, leading or cooperating with people, interviews, presentations or pitching ideas. See the *Flow* section in Chapter 10, Always Learning.

 Memory

Everything we experience through our lives is stored in our brain: everything we smell, touch, taste, see and hear, every sensation and piece of learning. It is our brain's job to interpret the light that reflects on to the lens of our eyes and the sound waves entering our brain; previous experience influences this interpretation. We all see, hear and interpret things differently. When our mind is interpreting information, it uses two types of memory: short-term and long-term.

Our short-term memory consists of pieces of information from our senses and our mind holds onto them briefly. This may be called our 'active memory'. Our short-term memory is like a processing unit; taking information from our senses, sorting it, interpreting it and storing it in our long-term memory.

The Impact of Memory

Some of the key conclusions that Dr. Wilder Penfield (a neurosurgeon from McGill University in Montreal) reached, after many years of research, are interesting for us to consider in relation to using visualisation and mental rehearsal to manage our thinking:

- The human brain acts in many ways like a video, vividly recording events. Whilst an event may not necessarily be easy to consciously retrieve by the individual, the event always exists in the brain.
- Both the event and the feelings experienced during that event are stored in the brain. The event and the feelings are locked together, and neither one can be recalled without the other.
- When an individual 'replays' their experiences, they can replay them in such a vivid form that they experience again the same emotions felt during the actual experience, not only remembering how they felt, but feeling the same way again.

We are able to use our short and long-term memories simultaneously. When we replay certain events, we are able to experience the emotions associated with those events whilst also being able to talk objectively about them. This has tremendous potential for us to learn and develop skills with systematic mental rehearsal. It also helps us to understand the positive or negative power of re-living positive and negative memories.

We have the power to re-wire; ditch (or at least minimise) that negative 'baggage', accumulated by reliving negative experiences, and reinforce the power of positive memories and results. We can also powerfully imagine and envision our future goals.

Our memories feed into our conscious and subconscious mind.

 Conscious and Subconscious Mind
The Basics

A man or woman who acquires the ability to take
full possession of his own mind
may take possession of anything else
to which he or she is justly entitled
Dale Carnegie

What is the Conscious Mind?

The conscious mind controls all the actions that we do intentionally, whilst being aware of what we're doing, or conscious; for example, when we decide to make any voluntary action, like picking up a glass. So, whenever we are aware of the thing we're doing, we are doing it with our conscious mind. The conscious mind can also be said to be the gate-keeper to the mind. If someone tries to present us with a belief that doesn't match our belief system, then our conscious mind will filter that belief. The same will happen when someone praises or criticises us; we'll filter that with our own reflection and through our previous experience and self-belief.

What is the Subconscious Mind?

The subconscious mind is the part of our brain responsible for all of our involuntary actions. Our breathing rate and heartbeats are controlled by our subconscious mind. Our emotions are also controlled by our subconscious mind. Our subconscious mind is also the place where our beliefs and memories are stored. Affirmations, for example, are done on a conscious level and are filtered by the subconscious mind if they don't match our belief system.

The way we can change a limiting belief is to convince the conscious mind logically to accept it so that it can pass to the subconscious mind and reside there.

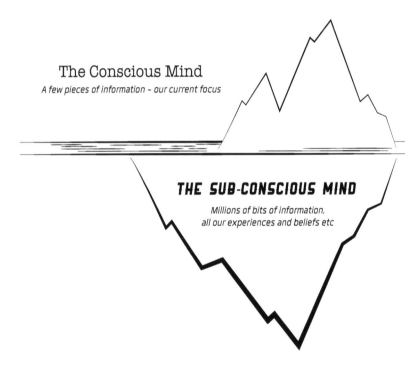

The Conscious Mind
A few pieces of information - our current focus

THE SUB-CONSCIOUS MIND

*Millions of bits of information,
all our experiences and beliefs etc*

Affirmations are a simple reminder to help this process. See definition and examples of affirmations in Chapter nine; Vision – Goals – Action page 114

Using the Conscious and the Subconscious Mind Together

Life is a mirror and will reflect back to
the thinker what he thinks into it.
Ernest Holmes

There is a simple exercise that we can do in order to understand the difference between the conscious and the subconscious mind.

If we start to control our breathing rate our conscious mind is in charge. Once we stop controlling our breathing and let it flow naturally, our subconscious mind takes over. In one experiment I undertook whilst I was linked to a heart rate monitor, I saw how I could clearly lower my heart rate by controlling my breathing, consciously affecting two usually subconscious processes. One benefit of understanding how both can be used together is the ability to control emotions. Since emotions are triggered by the subconscious mind, it's impossible to stop them. But knowing that the conscious mind processes thoughts, which are the primary trigger for emotions, we can learn to control our thoughts and, in turn, our emotions (particularly negative ones that disrupt us or hold us back), just as we can use meditation and mindfulness to lower our anxiety and stress and maintain our health.

 Think about a couple of events or achievements in your life: things for which you are responsible.

1. Recall a particularly thrilling event, something about which you feel very proud and positive. Notice how you can remember the event in vivid detail. Notice how you are probably smiling as you do so. Notice your body language when thinking about it. Notice how you are feeling.

2. Now think about an event that was negative. Something you don't want to repeat. Notice how you can recall this event in vivid detail. Notice how you are probably uncomfortable and frowning as you do so. Notice your body language when thinking about it. Notice how you are feeling.

Now imagine the power of each recollection on our self-belief and ability to confidently pursue our goals. If we want to achieve our positive future we need to focus on recalling the positives from our past, rather than allowing ourselves to be limited by the negative.

It is hard to fight an enemy who has
outposts in your head.
Sally Kempton

 # RAS – Reticular Activating System

Be careful what you wish for!

At this point, it's worth mentioning the reticular activating system (RAS). Our brain wants to help us get what we want, so we start to attract or see whatever we're focusing on – whether that's positive or negative! In simple terms, the RAS helps us spot the things that are important to us. It helps us focus on and attract the things we think about.

The R.A.S. also responds to novelty. We notice anything new and different and therefore adding novelty, colour, humour and interest to our goals, study or work can help us attract and remember things that are important to us.

We can programme our thoughts – every day – by focusing on what we want to achieve. There are thousands of pieces of information and potential stimuli around us all the time, and the RAS is the brain's way of helping us to focus on those things that are really important to us.

If ten of us walk down the same street we'll all notice different things, according to what we're thinking about, our different goals and how we've programmed our RAS.

It is therefore vital to:
- **Focus on what you want** rather than what you don't want.
- **Read/reflect on your long-term goals every day.**
- **Read/reflect on your short-term goals every day.**

This will help you spot those all-important opportunities that take you one step closer to achieving your goals in all areas of life: health, wealth and happiness.

Reminding ourselves of the bigger picture gets our brain focusing on what we want to achieve and prompts our RAS to spot opportunities to help us achieve them. Even when you don't realise you're thinking about these goals, your brain knows that they're important and takes note of anything that might help you to achieve them.

 Fight – Flight – Flock – Freeze

Our brain's natural survival mechanism and reaction to Fear – Anger – Stress

We all need to stay safe, be mindful of our own and our loved ones' survival, and instinctively react to protect ourselves. We are constantly interacting with the world, and every moment our brain is processing millions of information megabytes. It therefore has a kind of shorthand to help it with our survival. Some aspects of the brain are hardwired to enable us to respond to physical threat and danger.

Fear is a fundamental aspect of **survival**. Our brain's most important function is to keep us alive. It does so by regulating our heart rate, body temperature, and a myriad of other physiological functions, whilst also constantly scanning the environment for possible threats and rewards. Researchers such as Dr. Joseph LeDoux, and other researchers mentioned in his book, *The Emotional Brain*, have made huge contributions to the study of fear and its effect on the mind/body systems. He says: *'All animals have to protect themselves from dangerous situations in order to survive, and there are only a limited number of strategies that animals can call upon to deal with danger'.*

However, our natural, intuitive survival response can often become confused with fear or stress that is not linked to personal survival. When this happens in examinations, interviews, important performances or challenging situations, it causes stress, anger or anxiety that impedes our performance or prevents us from handling things effectively.

Every thought you have contributes to
truth or illusion; either it extends truth or it multiplies illusions.
Nothing but your own thoughts can hamper your progress.
Anonymous.

A danger or threat, physical or emotional, real or perceived, is recognised in the amygdala, and rather than sending information to our neocortex for processing and considered thought, information is then sent directly to the cerebellum, or 'reptilian brain', which produces our survival response. Great if we step out in front of a bus, not so good in a personal or professional situation where we want to handle things calmly and positively to bring about a positive outcome.

What Happens in Our Brain to Trigger Survival Mode?

Our survival instinct helps us to stay alive by triggering neurological pathways in our brain, which enable us to react to danger without even having to think about it.

Once our brain has decided there's a danger, it sends a flood of adrenaline, cortisol and other hormones that cause many changes in the body that include:

- heart rate and blood pressure rise;
- pupils dilate to take in as much light as possible;
- veins in skin constrict to send more blood to major muscle groups (responsible for the 'chill' sometimes associated with fear - less blood in the skin to keep it warm);
- blood-glucose levels increase;
- muscles tense up, energized by adrenaline and glucose (responsible for goose bumps - when tiny muscles attached

to each hair on the surface of the skin tense up, the hairs are forced upright, pulling skin with them);

- smooth muscle (that is responsible for the contractility of muscle in hollow organs) relaxes in order to allow more oxygen into the lungs;
- a burst of increased immunity;
- lower sensitivity to pain;
- non-essential systems (like digestion and immune system) shut down to allow more energy for emergency functions;
- heightened memory functions;
- trouble focusing on small tasks (brain is directed to focus only on the big picture in order to determine where the threat is coming from);
- lungs take in more oxygen and release more carbon dioxide;
- sweating increases to speed heat loss.

All of these physical responses are intended to help us survive in a dangerous situation by preparing us to predominantly either run for our life, or fight for our life. When our brain perceives a threat of any kind, it automatically responds in one of four modes. These are commonly known as **Fight, Flight, Flock, Freeze.** We don't usually choose these: we respond.

Fight

This is sometimes called defensive aggression. We feel in danger or threat and we start to fight. As we rarely need to tackle a predatory animal, there are few justifications for this in modern life. However, there are times when we might need the extraordinary bravery, strength and lower sensitivity to pain this gives us. For example, there are many examples of incredible bravery and strength on the part of parents protecting their children in danger.

However, we don't always use our fight responses when we're in actual physical danger. Our 'fight' response can be real fighting when we are younger; someone upsets us and we don't have the emotional control to manage it, or command of language to articulate our feelings without resorting to physical aggression. When my daughter was very young she used to hit out if she couldn't make herself understood, until she learned the necessary emotional control and command of language to explain herself. In those who don't learn to manage their responses, this can persist into teens and even adult life, to be addressed (or not) by anger management courses. This response can also be seen physically in adults on the sports field when their aggression becomes uncontrolled.

Too often, our 'fight' response emerges from non-physical threats: when we feel under pressure in tests, in work, in big performances have financial pressures, or during challenging times in personal relationships. We can become 'stressed' or 'defensive', which manifests itself as verbal aggression, rather than rational, considered discussions.

We can hang on to negative 'baggage' and allow this to cause issues in working and personal relationships, resulting in failure to resolve challenges that may then go on to become persistent causes of stress.

This is one reason why I believe in constant reflection to learn to handle things better: not to 'beat ourselves up', but to openly reflect and learn all the time to become more positive, more emotionally intelligent and therefore more able to effectively manage our memory bank.   The 2003 film *Anger Management* starring Jack Nicholson and Adam Sandler is a light-hearted look at this issue, with examples we can all relate to because we have all let our fight mechanism control us at some point, rather than us controlling it.

Flight

There are dangerous physical situations in which the safe course of action is to flee or run away. We flee a tsunami, a typhoon, a sand storm, an earthquake, a volcanic eruption, or similar natural disasters. Our brain tells us to run away when faced with overwhelming physical danger. In situations other than actual physical danger, flight is psychological rather than physical, and manifests itself in avoidance behavior: avoiding stating our views with someone who holds positional power over us, such as a teacher, boss or team coach; avoiding discussing topics we know will cause heated debate or confront issues with family or work colleagues; avoiding raising issues we may have with partners, friends or work colleagues.

Avoiding issues just leaves them unresolved, and we end up living with situations about which we are unhappy or resentful. It can also stop us from asking for clarity, which can limit our performance. Avoidance can certainly sour relationships or keep them going at a superficial level in a mode of permanent compromise. Flight responses link to the passive behaviour described in Chapter Fourteen, *Getting On Well With People*.

I have always thought it important to face things, even those things that are uncomfortable and cause debate. This is easier said than appropriately done but my experience is that letting things go needs to be a deliberate response for a specific reason, rather than a default mode. For example, if we let go too many things with our children when they're young, it becomes progressively more difficult to challenge behaviours that are unacceptable, or attitudes and behaviours that will hinder their progress, as they get older.

Flock

Traditionally, flock refers to the coming together of similarly threatened people, who then decide on an appropriate type of response to the fear context or threat scenario, such as protesting against oppression; joining together for strength. It also describes situations when individuals congregate in groups to positively support each other. However, it can also be a symptom of low self-regard and lack of confidence to need others around us with similar traits and can be a sign of passivity to feel safer by 'going with the crowd'.

Freeze

Another response to real or perceived danger is to 'freeze'. In a physical sense, this comes straight from the animal world, where it's designed to protect the animal from feeling pain during an attack; if an animal is lucky, the predator might think it is already dead and leave it. However, there are examples of people 'freezing' in extreme danger or a disaster, when the last thing they need to do is freeze. There are accounts of people in disasters totally incapable of thought or action and just needing to be directed.

In terms of perceived danger or fear, as opposed to real physical danger, we have all experienced the 'freeze' effects of our mind going blank in situations where we feel under pressure. We find some situations and events stressful, which can cause performance anxiety and freeze our thinking. These situations vary for individuals, according to the importance we place on them. Some people may 'freeze' in examinations, whilst others are capable of performing at their best. For some, it may be performances; such as sports, arts, interviews or public speaking. Whatever the situation, we can find ways to perform at our best when it matters most to us and overcome the debilitating effects of our natural 'auto-freeze' response.

It's important to note that this entire FIGHT, FLIGHT, FLOCK,
FREEZE survival process is automated; in other words,
our brain, or the neural pathways that are triggered,
determine how we will respond without us
consciously giving any real input.

BUT we can change the neural pathways we've developed
that produce responses which have a negative impact on us.

Acknowledge our fear. Accept our fear.
Don't let our fear control us. Conquer our fear.
Acknowledge our limiting, negative thinking and re-wire.

FEAR
The only thing we have to fear is fear itself.
Franklin D. Roosevelt

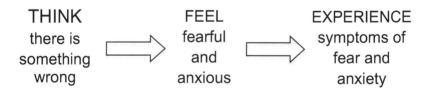

| THINK there is something wrong | → | FEEL fearful and anxious | → | EXPERIENCE symptoms of fear and anxiety |

Our survival reaction all comes down to our response to fear, whether real or perceived, and the anxiety that causes:

False
Expectations
Appearing
Real

The brain doesn't tend to recognise the difference between a real or an imaginary threat, e.g. running an imaginary argument or fight over in our mind causes stress, the sight of an exam paper or large household bill can cause stress, a bad dream reproduces the same physical affects as if what we're dreaming about is happening for real, and we all know what happens when two people in 'fight' mode clash! In this mode, we don't find solutions.

Firstly, we need to recognise times when we let our survival mode take over and get in the way. We can then train our mind to view things differently, and reduce the negative effects of worry, pressure and stress. Procrastination makes it worse. We benefit from acknowledging our fear but not allowing it to paralyse us. At times when we are feeling frightened, stressed or pressured we benefit from tackling challenges and issues, and having the courage to search for solutions. This is always easier said than done and we all find this more challenging sometimes than others. (And when you're expecting things of others, remember the situations we find challenging are different for different people!) If we recognise those times, without negative judgement, we can use the tools at our disposal to overcome our fears and anxiety. See the *Manage Stress (better)* chapter for more on this.

The bottom line is that we are all going to be frightened on occasions. If we want to thrive and succeed we have to be prepared to feel scared, acknowledge it and ignore it or deal with it. In her book *Daring Greatly: How The Courage To Be Vulnerable Transforms The Way We Live, Love, Parent And Lead,* Brené Brown suggests that, instead of letting fear stop you, it can help if we expect it to be there. Acknowledge it and, *'Say, 'I see you, I hear you, but I'll do this anyway'.'* She goes on to say, *'It feels dangerous to show up, but it's not as terrifying as thinking, at the end of our lives, 'What if I had shown up? What would have been different?'*

 How can we manage our thinking to improve the way we do things?

**Some men see things as they are and ask why.
Others dream things that never were and ask why not.**
George Bernard Shaw

Learning and Performing at Our Best

Our mind is where we learn, from formal education to experiential learning, and we can improve our capacity to learn, unlearn and re-learn by using it more effectively.

We can practise things in our mind to help us:
- o improve skills and embed learning in our neural pathways. (This is not a replacement for learning and technical skill development, but a way of improving skills, knowledge and understanding.);
- o 're-wire' our thinking; reinforcing positive thinking, self-belief and behaviours that help us achieve our goals and changing those negative, learned behaviours and beliefs that hold us back;
- o practise situations in our mind to help us perform at our best every day and when it matters most.

1. Learning new things and improving skills
We learn by creating neural pathways in our brain. For skill development, we need conscious repetition and deliberate practice in order to create those pathways. We can improve our execution of skills by mentally rehearsing the physical movement in our mind. We can mentally rehearse without the wear and tear on our bodies of physical practice (or the possible anxiety of others watching us fail!). In summary, to perfect execution and perform at our best, we need to repeatedly practise skills precisely and accurately and eliminate mistakes. Elite performers use their mind to help them do this.

Driving on the 'wrong' side of the road!

The most practical example I have of using my mind to learn and practise something is learning to drive on the 'wrong' side of the road. My first holiday abroad alone with my children, then aged 11 and 7, was to Mallorca, somewhere new for us all. After a scary attempt at hiring a car on our first visit, I was determined that we would explore the island on our next holiday.

How do you practise driving on the right in England, where we drive on the left? How do you practise driving a left-hand drive car when you don't have access to one? There's only one way, and that's in your mind. Using relaxation, visualisation and mental rehearsal every night for three weeks before travelling to Mallorca the following year, I learned to competently drive on the right in a right-hand drive car.

My children's obvious apprehension when we collected the car at the airport late at night was replaced by a stunned silence as I drove without hesitation and fairly competently. I'm not saying I drove with the unconscious competence I do at home, but safely enough for us to enjoy exploring the island, whilst not terrifying us or other road users.

2. Improving our ability to perform well in specific situations and when it matters most.

- When preparing to go into a challenging situation.
  If we mentally rehearse, focusing on it going well, things will dramatically improve.
- Preparing for study or work: thinking through what we want to achieve and how we're going to do it prepares our mind to perform well and enjoy it.
- Allowing our minds to flow rather than freeze, helps us to withdraw the right information when it matters most, even when we're under pressure and in competitive situations, such as exams, interviews and important performances.

- Using our imagination to positively rehearse situations we have not experienced before is also valuable.

3. Improving our ability to manage relationships

Managing our mind, rather than just reacting, helps us with one of the most important aspects of our lives, the way we relate with others. In family, personal, social and work situations we can continuously improve the way we handle our relationships with others. It's amazing what a difference it can make if we improve our handing of those tricky discussions (personal and professional) by preparing to be positive, confident, assertive, conciliatory and focused on positive outcomes, rather than limited by constant replays that reinforce negative prior experiences. Mentally rehearsing scenarios and situations takes practise but has amazing results.

4. Creating Positive Habits

Habits are repeated behaviours. These are created in our neural pathways and we can help create and reinforce positive habits and eliminate negative habits by focused mental rehearsal. Establishing new habits is easier for some than others. Overcoming limiting, negative thinking can take a while for many of us! It all depends on how engrained our old habits are, how open-minded we are and how well we have established our growth mindset.

We are what we repeatedly do.
Excellence, therefore, is not an act but a habit.
Aristotle

Everything we do starts with a thought, and successful people have a growth mindset, generate positive thoughts and keep their mind focused on the most important things.

5. Creative Thinking - Improving Our Ability to Find Solutions

People like Leonardo da Vinci and Albert Einstein were masters of using the power of their mind to find creative solutions. Using the creative powers of our imagination and maintaining a positive, can-do, growth mindset can be the difference between rising to a challenge, or being overwhelmed.

Creativity goes beyond knowledge recall and extends into knowledge creation. Using our imagination and creativity helps us to 'create' the future we want, see the best path for us, and handle challenges. It is important to combine our imagination and creativity with our knowledge and experience to perform at our best.

Imagination is more important than knowledge
Albert Einstein

Sometimes, we have vast knowledge in a field and finding improvement comes from another field: business learns from sport; sport learns from sciences, and so on. Original ideas are often created by blending concepts from different fields into something new, as demonstrated by the greatest thinkers.

However, in order to use other ideas and concepts it helps to let our imagination and creativity flow. For this, we need space, 'head space', away from the myriad of demands we have around us. Consequently, people who use the power of their mind recognise the importance of

intuition   instinct   imagination

as well as facts, logic and analysis.

Trust yourself: your belief, skill, instinct, knowledge and intuition. It makes a tremendous, positive difference if we go into things with belief in ourselves and belief in our capacity to make the right decisions.

If we allow pressure to 'freeze' our brain, or the way some put it, 'let our nerves get to us', our judgement goes. Keeping our brain in flow to access our accumulated knowledge and experience and use our intuition and imagination gives us the best chance of realising our potential and achieving our goals. We can learn to do this by managing our mind: relaxing and focusing to allow our mind to make the right connections to plan, create, perform and make those all-important decisions.

> *Creativity is seeing what others see and*
> *thinking what no one else has ever thought.*
> Albert Einstein

> *Creativity can solve almost any problem. The creative act, the*
> *defeat of habit by originality, overcomes everything.*
> George Lois

6. Focus and Discipline

Focus and discipline serve us in whatever we want to achieve. They are natural partners with curiosity and creative flow, and an important part of us developing our persistence and resilience.

Think about when you first learned something, for example, riding a bicycle: how difficult it was, and how you kept practising, falling off, and practising again until your brain could tell your body how to do it well. You could then cycle without having to think about how to do it. So it is with everything – learning new skills, learning how to do things better, changing negative habits to positive habits, overcoming fear and using your creativity all require repeated, disciplined practise until they become natural for us.

7. Developing Our Winning Mentality

This doesn't mean a 'win-at-all-cost' mentality but the focused, disciplined action, self-belief, creativity, ability to handle pressure and perform at our best when it matters most, reflection and review that enables us to achieve constant and never-ending improvement. A belief in CANI – **C**onstant **A**nd **N**ever-ending **I**mprovement, is a thread that weaves its way through equipped2succeed.

Defining a winning mentality:

> **One's ability to maximise one's potential,**
> **even under pressure**
> **and in competitive situations.**

What's important to realise our potential is to perform at our best when it matters most. Training our mind is one of the ways we can ensure that happens.

'She / he's always in control' (not to be confused with controlling) is a phrase often used about winners or high achievers in any context. Winners are able to control their emotional state when it matters most and think correctly or clearly under pressure, not allowing themselves to be limited or paralysed by fear. They manage to flow rather than freeze under pressure. Winners **T.C.U.P.**

Think **C**orrectly (Clearly) **U**nder **P**ressure

When under pressure, we always have more time than we feel or think we have. We hear individuals talk about having more time than they thought in tests or examinations, when their minds are in flow and they are recalling all the information they need. In order to practice T.C.U.P. and perform at our best under pressure, we can train our mind to flow rather than freeze. Trust our skills, trust our knowledge, trust our experience, trust our ability to handle challenge and allow all our learning to flow to enable us to perform at our best when it matters most.

 ## Using Our Minds to Manage Our Thinking and Improve Our Performance

Relaxation – Visualisation – Mental Rehearsal

Relaxation, Visualisation and Mental Rehearsal is our own personal programming technique. Relaxing, visualising and rehearsing things in our mind is an invaluable technique. Variations of this process are proven to work in sports, and are used, in their own unique way, by all those who succeed in their chosen field, including all 500 leaders interviewed by Napoleon Hill in the 1930's for his book, *'Think and Grow Rich'*.

We can help to build and maintain our ability and belief to perform at our best and achieve our goals by doing our own programming.

A key aspect of the process is the act of regarding what's in our mind as an objective reality. Sally Gunnell's book, *'Be Your Best'*, contains one of the most powerful accounts I have read of the power of the mind and this process. Sally recounts her preparation and performance at the 1992 Barcelona Olympics. Although this is a sporting experience, we can recognise the power of the way she programmed her thinking and apply if for ourselves.

'Let me explain why I believe in the power of the mind so completely. Barcelona 1992: a world-class mind-game. Ten months before the 1992 Olympics in Barcelona, my chances of winning a gold medal looked slim...they said I wasn't tough enough to win.

Luckily, their negativity just made me think: "Right! I'll show you!" Instead of quitting, I searched even harder for advice on preparation. I visited the 1968 Olympic champion of the 400m hurdles, David Hemery, to find out how he achieved his magnificent victory. He told me to visualize. "Oh, I do that already, the night before a race," I told him. "I go through it all in my mind so I'm mentally prepared." "No I mean really visualise," he said. "Every day, several times a day, I want you to go through every aspect of the 400m hurdles Olympic final in your mind, from the instant the gun fires to the moment you cross the line. I want you to imagine every possible race scenario. I want you to stand next to every possible competitor, with different athletes ahead at different stages. Only one thing must always be the same: you must always win."

So I did. Every day, eight or ten times a day, I went through that race in my mind. I did it while I ran; I did it lying down with my eyes shut. Sometimes the imaginary me made a mistake, so I'd see myself correcting it and carrying on. Sometimes I'd nearly get to the end and find I wasn't in front, so I had to rewind and play it again to make sure I was. I must have run that final more than 2000 times before I lined up for it on a warm evening in Barcelona'.

Sally Gunnell went on to win Gold and says: 'Seventy per cent of that race was won by my mind. From then on, I was totally sold on mental techniques and I continued to learn more about their potential. **Visualisation is not a magic potion you can only use once and never again, it's the ultimate 'use it or lose it'. The more you practise, the better it gets**, as I found a year later, before the World Championships.'

We can apply the techniques Sally used to be our best in every aspect of our lives. We can use a R – V – MR process to help our discipline, focus and confidence; improve skills; improve every-day life and relationships; reduce stress and perform under pressure; help us to be more creative and achieve our big goals. It can be used to improve every aspect of our wellbeing and performance.

equipped2succeed

e2s - **R**elaxation – **V**isualisation – **M**ental **R**ehearsal Process

*Life is a mirror and will reflect back to
the thinker what he thinks into it.*
Ernest Holmes

Step 1 Relaxation

enables our mind to be quiet and focus.
Effective relaxation relieves stress, tension and anxiety. Systematically relaxing enables us to be mindful, be creative and focus our thinking on what we want to achieve. Relaxation allows our brain to make the right connections, helping our minds to flow and focus on what we want to achieve.

Some of us can relax and quieten our mind more easily than others. After years of practice I know the benefits, but still find quietening my mind more challenging than some people.
It is also very difficult to go through any form of systematic relaxation if we are full of stimulants, such as caffeine.

Step 2 Visualisation

enables us to imagine what we want to achieve and how we want to perform.

Visualisation enables us to go on a mental journey into our imagination, where we can tune into the power of our mind to see ourselves achieving. Imagine the scene in your mind and see
yourself in bright technicolour saying what you want to say, being clams and focused, responding appropriately to others or performing at your peak in your chosen endeavour. We can watch our preferred version of events happen, again and again, like action replays.

Step 3 Mental Rehearsal

enables us to use our mind to practise our skills, interactions and performance.

Through mental rehearsal, we can see, feel and hear ourselves achieving our goals. We can practise things in our mind, create scenarios and achieve, the positive outcomes we are seeking, reinforcing whatever we've learned and preparing for important situations. We can rewind and do it better: improving our performance, designing the future we choose and celebrating our achievements.

Find a summary of this process and guided R – V – MR in the free resources on www.equipped2succeed.co.uk

You can download music and guided R-V-MR tracks, especially designed to help you establish your own process.

With consistent practice this process becomes an invaluable tool.

Use the power of your mind to perform at your best.

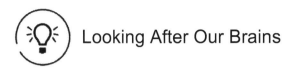 Looking After Our Brains

**The brain represents 3% of the body's weight
and uses 20% of the body's energy.**

There is a lot we can do to look after our brain. The majority of the energy consumed by the brain powers the rapid firing of the billions of neurons communicating with each other. The rest of its energy is used for controlling other activities, both unconscious activities, such as heart rate, and conscious ones, such as studying, working or driving a car. At any given moment, not all of the brain's regions are concurrently firing. However, brain researchers using imaging technology have shown that, like the body's muscles, most are continually active over a 24-hour period. Even in sleep, areas such as the frontal cortex, which controls things like higher-level thinking and self-awareness, are active. What is clear from all the research is that we need to look after our brain if we want it to perform at its best.

Eating healthily: particular 'brain foods' that are recognised to help our brain's function include: oily fish, blueberries, blackcurrants, pumpkin seeds, tomatoes, broccoli, sage and nuts.

Drinking plenty of water: water is essential for our brain to work effectively. Research consistently proves that drinking water improves brain functioning. It's no coincidence that a headache is a sign of being dehydrated.

Exercising: our brain loves to move. Exercise helps get more essential oxygen to our brain, stimulates positive endorphins and improves our ability to think clearly.

More on being D.E.A.R. to ourselves (**D**iet – **E**xercise – **A**ttitude – **R**est) in Chapter thirteen, *Maximise Energy*.

**Our thinking improves the more we use, stimulate and
expand our mind.**

*Iron rusts from disuse; water loses its purity from stagnation...
even so does inaction sap the vigour of the mind.*
Leonardo da Vinci

 ACTION

Every day give yourself a good mental shampoo.
Dr. Sara Jordan

Use Relaxation – Visualisation – Mental Rehearsal to:

- exercise your imagination;
- think positively;
- practise your skills;
- rehearse your day going how you want it to go;
- rehearse a lesson or session;
- rehearse an important performance;
- manage relationships; be at your best and bring out the best in others;
- overcome fears;
- achieve your goals, the things that are really important to you – things you want to BE – HAVE – DO.

Use meditation to improve your ability to manage stress, be mindful and be well. *Headspace* is my favourite App for this.

*Nothing but your own thoughts
can hamper your progress.*
Anon

CHOOSE YOUR THOUGHTS

Chapter Seven

Being Positive

Positive thinking, language and behaviours to achieve positive outcomes.

positive: *confident in opinion or assertion; fully assured; emphasizing what is hopeful, or to the good; constructive: a positive attitude toward the future; possessing an actual force, being, existence; constructive and sure, rather than sceptical; showing or expressing approval or agreement; full of confidence, or giving cause for hope and confidence.*

Let's start with a challenge. Whenever I start a workshop focused on positive mental attitude participants often question the concept of being relentlessly positive. It's challenging: some are sceptical and most of us naturally look for things to be easier. Marc and Angel's quote is part of the response to that challenge:

> ***Being positive doesn't mean ignoring the negative. Being positive means overcoming the negative. There's a big difference between the two.***

This chapter explores why being positive is important and how we can consistently develop and maintain the positivity that will serve us well. It is challenging. Every day I find myself with unhelpful negative thoughts that I need to rewind and reframe to limit their impact.

I love the title of Emeli Sande's track, *Our Version of Events*, because that's exactly what we want our future to be: we need to be able to create our own future. And surely we want our future to be positive, have a positive impact with those around us, and a positive impact in the endeavours and causes we hold D.E.A.R.? No matter what we do in life, a positive mindset, positive thinking, positive language and positive feelings bring better outcomes for us, and those around us. Much of this book is about the way we think and how that affects our potential to achieve. We attract into our lives the things we think about, whether they're positive or negative; so surely we want the positive version?

Our mindset influences everything we do
and we can choose our mindset.

This the last of human freedoms – to choose one's attitude in any given set of circumstances, to choose one's own way.
Viktor Frankl
Concentration Camp survivor and author of
Man's Search for Meaning.

We can choose the way we are in every situation, and approaching people, goals and tasks with a positive mindset has tremendous benefits in all areas of life.

Relationships: being positive with family, in personal and professional relationships, with those we come into contact with in leisure interests, as well as those people you come into contact with on a casual basis improves life. No matter who we interact with, about what, being positive is better for everyone involved.

Whoever is happy will make others happy too.
Anne Frank

Goals: decide and articulate what you want, not what you don't want. Having specific goals and being positive and enthusiastic about achieving them will help us attract all the help we need.

Learning: we get much more from formal study and informal learning if we approach it with a positive, open mindset – one that appreciates the joy of learning and the benefits for us.

Work: if we find the positive in our work, and are positive with others we will reap the rewards with colleagues, with increased satisfaction and success.

Interests: whether our interests are sports, music, art or technology, we will have more fun, achieve much more and gain more satisfaction with a positive mindset. If we can't be positive about our interests, perhaps we're pursuing the wrong ones. Let's avoid being that angry, energy sapper in the team!

Positive Mental Attitude: P.M.A.

Having a positive attitude and outlook is essential for success in any field. Research shows that elite athletes and successful business people alike all share a relentlessly positive mental attitude (PMA). Colin Jackson, was a world champion hurdler, and is now a successful athletics (track and field) commentator. When tested, he was off the scale with his positive attitude. That's what helped him become an Olympic medallist, world champion, world record holder, a successful TV Commentator, and an exceptional competitor on the UK's *Strictly Come Dancing*.

Focusing our thinking on the positive things we want, rather than dwelling on the negative things we don't want, is essential for success. The reticular activating system in our brains actually focuses on attracting what we think about, and we want to attract the positive version of events. Being positive helps us in specific endeavours. It also helps us to achieve holistic success in living a happy, fulfilled life; enjoying every day, being grateful, relishing every experience and finding the positive in our experiences.

It's not our environment or what happens to us that determines our attitude, but rather how we respond to our situation.

A positive attitude gives you power over your circumstances instead of your circumstances having power over you.
Joyce Meyer

Charles Swindoll sums it up very well:

The remarkable thing we have is a choice every day regarding the attitude we will embrace for that day.
We cannot change our past.
We cannot change the fact that people will act in a certain way.
We cannot change the inevitable.
The only thing we can do is play on the one string we have, and that is our attitude.

Some of the most successful people have used a positive mental attitude to get them through very challenging life experiences as well as to enable them to make the most of opportunities in their field: business leaders, charity leaders, sports people, leading politicians, actors, musicians, successful people in every field of endeavour.

There are some key things to consider when seeking to improve and maintain a positive mindset and positive feelings. We need to maintain positive language. Our emotional state affects everything we are and everything we do. Therefore, the way we feel has a powerful impact on what happens and what we can achieve in all areas of our life.

Our mindset and language influences our emotional state and that of those around us. The way we think and communicate with ourselves and others affects the way we feel, and vice versa, so if we are going to achieve and be happy, we need to ensure that positive emotions and feelings predominate in our thinking and language. These can be summarised as:

Enjoyment: happiness, joy, relief, contentment, bliss, delight, amusement, pride, sensual pleasure, thrill, rapture, gratification, satisfaction, euphoria;

Love: acceptance, friendliness, trust, kindness, affinity, devotion, adoration;

Surprise: astonishment, amazement, wonder.

Our feelings drive us and determine our momentum towards our goals. To continue the driving analogy, our feelings enable us to balance our life through the gears. We don't want to be stuck in reverse or neutral. However, if we drive in fifth gear all the time, we will burn out.

We are all going to suffer sadness, anger and a whole host of negative emotions from time to time. We feel sadness when we suffer loss, but it's essential for our wellbeing that we accept it, without letting it overwhelm us for too long. We will also feel angry about things sometimes. Firstly, we need to reflect and think whether or not it's something important enough for us to be angry about. All too often, I meet people who are angry frequently about many small things. Secondly, if it's something that means a lot to us, we must either do something about it or let it go. If you can do something about it, just do it (as the advert says). If you can't do anything about it, just let it go. Hanging on to negative emotions drains our energy, makes us anxious and blocks us from focusing our all-important energy and feelings on the positive things in our lives. It's challenging, but crucial, to find the positive and focus our attention on the positives in people, the positives in our lives, and the outcomes we want.

Moving Through Our Gears!

Reverse	"Woe is me." Negative feelings & language keep us in a negative cycle. Bored. Can't be bothered.
Neutral	Rest from the other gears! In danger of stalling! Don't know. Stuck. Unable to move forward. Telling ourselves we're getting nowhere. Lack of focus and direction.
1st	Moving forward slowly, on one thing at a time. Limited to focusing on one thing at once.
2nd	Picking up pace on achieving our goals.
3rd	Starting to implement plans in a more disciplined, determined way.
4th	Moving forward on all our goals in a systematic way.
5th	Full speed ahead on all our goals. Taking disciplined, focused action every day. Maintaining balance means we need to use neutral to ensure we rest enough, keeping our energy for the important things.

We all want to reach a more consistent state of 'cruise control', more efficient and using less of our valuable energy.

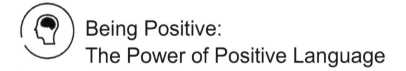

Being Positive:
The Power of Positive Language

There are three main aspects of language that we need to think about when improving our positive mindset.

What We Say to Others: The Language We Use

Framing our language in the positive is vital. That means saying what you do want, not what you don't want.

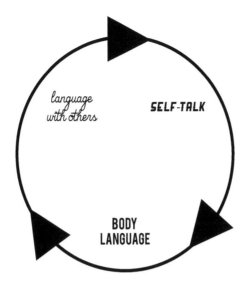

Find the positive in situations and experiences and be grateful. Express yourself positively: value experiences and value those around you. NB If we can't value individuals in our lives because of the negative impact they have on us we need to minimise their impact on us or not have them in our lives anymore.

Much of the issue with negative language is starting a phrase with 'don't'. Our brains don't really hear or register the 'don't', and therefore just hear the rest of the sentence as a command, and the behavior we're looking to modify continues. That's why we hear ourselves saying, 'I've told him / her over and over again not to do that'.

We need to say what we do want, not what we don't.

There are times when we need to challenge an individual's behaviour or attitude, and, whilst it's essential to assertively address issues, rather than leave them to be even more draining, it's always best to do this in a positive way. Find a positive, be explicit about what you want them to improve, then end with a positive. This way we focus on improvement, rather than criticism, in a way that people can take it on board without it affecting their self-regard. There's more on the impact of our language on self-regard in Chapter eleven: *The Power of Self-Belief.*

What We Say to Ourselves: Our Self-Talk

He who thinks he can or he who thinks
he can't, are both usually right.
Confucius

Self-talk refers to the ongoing internal conversation we hold with ourselves, which influences how we feel and behave. Self-talk is the most powerful of language in influencing our behaviour and what we achieve.

Negative self-talk is characterised by thinking such as:

I can't.
I'm never going to get this done in time.
This test is going to be too difficult for me. I'm never going to pass.
I knew this would be a bad day as soon as I was late. (You knew it, so it was like that!)

Positive self-talk is characterised by thinking such as:

I can.
I'll get this done in time. It will be a challenge, but I can do it.
This test will be challenging, but I know I'm good enough to pass. I will pass.
I knew I would make the time up after being late.'(You knew it, so it was like that!)

The Power of Gratitude

The greatest discovery of any generation is that
human beings can alter their lives by altering
the attitudes of their minds.
Albert Schweitzer

One of the best ways of maintaining our positive self-talk is by practising gratitude. For me, this is powerfully described in Rhonda Byrne's inspiring film and books, *The Secret* and *The Power*. In brief, practising gratitude is reflecting on the things we are grateful for: family, health, friends, wealth, and abundance in our lives.

By focusing on what we have, we radiate positive thoughts of abundance and create those all-important good feelings that help us move on to achieve what we really want.

Body Language

We can change the way we think and feel by changing our body language, and this also has an enormous effect on the way we are received by people.

Why is body language so important?

Research undertaken at the University of Pennsylvania set out to determine to what extent a person's body language can affect the impression people form of him/her. The surprising result was that body language was found to be more responsible for the impression people form of you than your words. Here are some of the findings they came up with regarding the impression people form of you:

- 55% is based on your postures, body movements and gestures;
- 38% is based on the tone of your voice (tempo and pitch);
- only 7% is based on what you say.

This means that a total of 93% of the impression people form of you is determined by your **body language** (which includes both body gestures and voice tone), whilst only 7% is based on the words you speak.

Now, consider what impact your body language has on you and those around you. Think about how you feel when using positive and negative body language.

Positive body language is smooth, balanced, firm and open, characterised by:

       appropriate eye contact (dependent on culture);
       smiling;
       'smiling' eyes;
       open posture;
       standing tall (without being intimidating);

enthusiastic gestures;
body language in tune with what you say;
body language appropriate to the environment / situation.

> ***A smile is a light in the window of the
> soul indicating that the heart is home.***
> Anonymous

Negative Body Language can take lots of forms, but the most common forms involve either submission or aggression:

Submissive body language is characterised by:
hunching inwards;
head tilting downwards;
stillness;
smiling with your mouth, but not your eyes.

Aggressive body language is characterised by:
disapproving facial expressions (frowning);
sighing;
invading personal space;
large gestures.

 I am very aware that my feelings are near the surface, and I have needed to work very hard to reduce and reframe criticism and disapproval.

I have needed to learn to consciously frame issues in a way that focuses on challenging individuals to improve, focusing on positive outcomes, rather than criticism that leaves people feeling negative. My negative body language was 'sighing', which is heavily weighted with disapproval. It makes people feel much worse than clearly explaining the issue and seeking to find a solution. I am on a continuous mission to address this, and would like to take this opportunity to apologise to anyone who has 'felt' my sigh, especially my children.

How we receive what others say to us

Just as it's important to be positive in what we say, it's equally important to receive what others say in a positive way. This doesn't mean agreeing with everything, but responding in an open, non-judgmental way.

Ensuring we receive what others say positively starts with listening actively.

Positive, active listening makes people feel we're interested and enables us to really hear what they say. It is vital for those around us to feel they are listened to and heard by us.

Negative, disinterested listening makes people feel we're not interested; as a result we miss things and misunderstand what is being communicated.

There are times when we have other pressing priorities, and we really don't have the time to listen to a long story. In this case, we should say that we are interested, but have 'x' (be specific rather than just saying busy – people appreciate this!) to do; and agree a time when we *can* listen. Of course, this is not so useful with little people who want to tell you NOW!

How do you feel when someone is obviously not listening to, or hearing, what you say? Ensure you do everything you can to not let others feel this way.

It is very important that we surround ourselves with positive people protect ourselves from negativity and challenge negativity if we are to develop a consistently positive mental attitude. To do this sometimes we need to take the lead in modeling positive, helpful thinking, language and behaviours.

Two things to remember when considering how we can enable people around us to think positively:

Mirroring: individuals will mirror our language if we say it confidently and assertively.

Modelling: individuals follow our model if we say it confidently and assertively.

In all this, it is worth keeping in mind that even if you behave a certain way only 40% of the time, people will perceive you as behaving that way all of the time!

A positive attitude is like a fire: unless you continue to add fuel, it goes out.
Alexander Lockheart

Personal Energy

Be a fountain, not a drain.
Rex Hudler

At this point, it's worth mentioning that we all have energy around us, and it is either positive or negative. It can, and does, affect others. Those of us who are more able to tune into other's feelings may feel the positive and negative energy of others more acutely. However, most of us have walked into a room and felt the negative tension or the positive warmth, the anger or the enthusiasm. What we need to be aiming for is to create positive energy and protect ourselves from negative energy.

We have all met people who are energy givers: who radiate positive energy and who make you feel better by spending time with them. We've also met those who are energy sappers: who drain our energy with their negativity if we don't protect ourselves. The term 'mood hoover' illustrates this very well.

Energy Givers and Energy Sappers

There are positive people who, by the sheer nature of their positive attitude and energy, give you energy. That doesn't mean people who are ingratiatingly 'nice' or complement everything we do. Energy givers may be challenging but they are coming from a positive standpoint of wanting us to be the best version of ourselves, achieve our dreams and goals, and know that some positive challenge is required to do that. They also radiate positivity that is infectious.

Then there are the energy sappers, or 'mood hoovers'. They are negative, have a 'BUT' for every positive idea or solution and, if we allow them, soak up our positive energy and leave us drained. We need to remove the energy sappers from our circle or, if they are family, make sure our protective force field is intact and strong. My failure in this area has been that, by the nature of my 'can always improve' instinct and desire for people to be their best, I have too often tried to change those people around me. Many times, it would have been better to accept what I could not change and focus on protecting myself, and on things over which I could actually have some positive influence.

Sometimes, we may choose to associate with the energy sappers because they are close family members or close childhood friends who, despite everything, we want to help. If this is the case we need to ensure that our protection mechanisms are in place. Again, very successful people have in-built natural protection and are generally better at not letting him or her 'get to them'; and you'll rarely hear a successful person say '*s/he does my head in'*. They just don't let people negatively affect them. Naturally, they have a better in-built force field or protective 'bubble' and they deliberately hone this over time. It has certainly taken me many years to develop mine, and I still have to very consciously pull it on or wrap it around me when the 'mood hoovers' are around.

We all need our own invisible 'bubble' to let all the positives in and let the negatives bounce off us. Sometimes, we do this the other way around: hear the negatives and not the praise, which damages our mood, our positive self-image, our self-regard and self-belief.

Use the Positive and Dispel the Negative.
Creating Our Own Protective Bubble or Protective Force-field.

My children say I live in my own 'bubble'.

After years of practice, I am very highly tuned to people's positive or negative state, and as soon as they slip into negativity, my 'bubble' comes on and I endeavour to ensure all the negativity bounces off (not always successfully, but then I am human and sensitive to others!). I actively listen, I empathise, I endeavour to find the positives, I try to help them find solutions, but I don't allow their negative toxicity to drain me. I have taken on other's challenges many times over the years at an enormous cost to my own wellbeing. That doesn't mean I'm not challenging and I'm certainly still on my journey to being relentlessly positive. I am always seeking improvement and endeavour to find solutions. I try to find language to frame this in a way that doesn't come across as implicit criticism. If I slip into negativity the look on my children's, friend's and colleague's faces swiftly brings me back to reframing my thinking in the positive. Isn't it great when those around us reflect back to us in a way that's helpful?

Our positive protection bubble can be whatever image we want around us. Some people conjure up a clear bubble like the ones you blew from a little plastic bottle when you were a child; others visualise some form of forcefield, and some an umbrella. Seve Ballesteros, one of the greatest golfers of all time, talked about being in his bubble on the tee and not letting any negativity affect him. It is a visual representation of what we need to do in our mind when confronted by people who will drain our energy, positivity and confidence, if we allow it.

**Just like anything else in life – with positive thinking,
you get out what you put in.**

Being optimistic and positive about what we, and those around us, can achieve is essential. The negative alternative simply doesn't make any sense! Having high expectations of ourselves and those around us builds positive momentum. From experience, I have learned that most people live up to, or down to, the expectations of those around them. It therefore makes sense to find the positive in others and support those around us to improve.

Say positive things to people and you get positive comments back.

Adopt positive body language and you'll feel more positive and get positive responses from others.

Receive what others say positively and actively listen, and people will respond positively to you and actively listen to you.

The most important and most challenging thing is positive thinking and self-talk. Frame thinking in the positive and we'll feel, and be, more able to achieve what we want to be, do and have.

We therefore need to tell ourselves, and others, about what we want to happen rather than what we don't want to happen: frame everything we say, and think about, in the positive. Whatever we say and think about adds to its power, whether that is positive or negative, and we surely want to be always adding power to the positive.

Remember: our subconscious mind believes what we tell it. So we need to put in what we want to get out.

For example:
'I'm tired': say it ten times and, low and behold, you're feeling more tired. You shouldn't deny reality, but by replacing 'I'm tired' with 'I could have more energy' you are positively telling yourself how you want to feel rather than making yourself more tired.

'Do's' rather than 'Don'ts'
We need to tell others what we want and avoid saying what we don't want.

'I hate ....' Using the word 'hate' is very negative, and projecting extreme negativity affects us in a negative way. Whether we dwell on positive or negative emotions, we add to their power. Isn't it much more helpful for us all to add power to the positive?

Please don't confuse positive with passive and easy. Positive people can be very challenging of themselves and those around them, but they can still be energy givers. If positivity is combined with goals, ambition and competitiveness, positive people can be very demanding. The fact that they are positive can make them more demanding because they are less easy to ignore. It's far easier for people to put barriers up, and not engage with the moaner, the person who's very unfair, the person who's always finding fault: the energy sapper. This is much more difficult with the positive person,
who challenges those around them to go that bit further, to do that bit better, and to practice C.A.N.I. (Constant And Never-ending Improvement).

The optimist lives on the peninsula of infinite possibilities; the pessimist is stranded on the island of perpetual indecision.
William Ward

 Positivity Health Warnings!

Internal Negativity: Why worry? What does worry achieve?

Ben Howard suggests that fear creates worry in his track *The Fear*:
'I've been worrying that we all live our lives in the confines of fear'.
We can spend too much of our time fearing and worrying about what we don't want. As we attract what we think about, the more we worry about something, the more likely we are to realise the negative outcomes we fear. Simply dwelling on what we fear attracts it to us. How many times have we all said to ourselves something like, 'I knew today wouldn't go well', and we 'achieved' that self-fulfilling prophecy. We can so easily end up in a negative cycle, and surely, we all want to live in a positive cycle?

Worry is Weighty and Worthless

 Although my natural self is a positive, enthusiastic one, I have found myself, at times, in the negative worry cycle, and it's not a good place to be.

When I was an Area Education Officer, Alan, one of the Deputies repeatedly said to me, 'Beverley, worry is worthless baggage'. He had to say it quite a few times for it to become one of my mantras. What good does worry do? None. It doesn't solve anything. With all the negative emotions that go with it, worry just emotionally and physically drains us. However, not worrying doesn't mean not taking responsibility. But taking responsibility is finding solutions to challenges, finding positive outcomes, and worry, by its very nature, is negatively dwelling on negative outcomes. So, guess what? If that's what we do, that's what we get.

External Negativity

Keep your 'bubble' securely around you when faced with negativity from others. Don't let negativity penetrate when faced with those who catastrophise things: the 'cynical sods' and the '1001 reasons why not guys'.

Moaning as a Pass-time – 'Catastrophising Stuff'

We can all do this on occasion, but there are those who consistently moan and 'catastrophise' things: who often talk about challenges as issues and problems, and constantly re-frame them for different audiences, creating melodrama with their tone of voice and body language. Each time they repeat or moan about the issue it is re-enforced in their mind. They repeat it lots, internally and with others, in different ways, to different people who often build on the negative aspects of the issue. The grooves of doom and gloom become well-formed and embedded in their brain. Sometimes, the magnitude of something that is quite minor grows as the heart-felt negative emotion attached to it takes hold. Sometimes, the original story is someone else's, but by repeating it, the teller takes on the negativity within it.

Spending today moaning about yesterday
won't make tomorrow any better!

Dwelling on the negative simply contributes to its power.
Shirley MacLaine

'Cynical Sods'

There are those who are cynical; they see the negative in every situation, always assume the worst, and tell everyone it won't work, whatever the 'it' is. You can spot them in groups in all walks of life. We cannot always avoid the cynics; they may be family members, individuals in our class or team, or people we work with. However, they are definitely energy sappers, rather than energy givers, and it is vital that our bubble is reinforced against their toxic negativity.

We can become bitter or better as a result of our experiences.
Eric Butterworth

'1001 Reasons Why Not Brigade'

One of the recurring themes in this book is that successful people take action, are creative and find solutions. They DO THE WORK. They pursue their goals, train, learn what they need to learn, and find the people who can help them. By contrast, we have all met those people who do everything they can to avoid change and the effort that entails: who protect the status quo and do everything they can to stay within their ever-shrinking comfort zone. They will always give you 1001 reasons why not to do something. They often call themselves realists and brand others (very often me!) as idealists. There are also those who live in a 'paralysis of analysis' that prevents them from having the courage take action and build the momentum to keep moving forward.

A Native American grandfather was talking to his grandson
about how he felt.
He said, "I feel as if I have two wolves fighting in my heart.
One wolf is the vengeful, angry, violent one.
The other wolf is the loving, compassionate one."
The grandson asked him, "
Which wolf will win the fight in your heart?"
The grandfather answered: "The one I feed."

The pessimist sees difficulty in every opportunity.
The optimist sees the opportunity in every difficulty.
Winston Churchill

I have experienced the power of positive thinking in some of my most challenging times, in achieving my goals, with my children, and with individuals in limiting, negative environments. I always endeavour to be positive, dwell on and be grateful for the positives and learn from the mistakes, negatives and sadness that we all face at times.

Negative situations often offer more opportunity for us to learn if we're prepared to reflect, review, reframe, change and grow. This doesn't mean that I haven't challenged myself, and others, to improve and take responsibility for their performance. I have just framed it in learning and positive development, rather than being limited by negativity.

Remaining Positive, Even in the Face of Adversity Focusing on Positive Outcomes

 Anyone can be positive when things are going well. What's important is to find that positive force within you, even when things are at their worst.

Like many people, the most negative time of my life was separation and divorce. I was angry, upset, and full of all those negative emotions you experience when you feel as if you were supposed to be married for life and then, suddenly, you're not.

I don't want to share the details of my separation and divorce here. That would not serve anyone involved, me, my children, my children's father or his wife and children. What I do want to say is that, after fighting for a year to save my marriage, I finally realised that, no matter how much I tried to change it was broken beyond repair, and I made a conscious decision to move on without malice and not put my 'baggage' onto my children. I had seen too many families torn apart, not by divorce, but by the aftermath of divorce. I decided that we had two fabulous children together and I needed to make our future relationship work for them (and me). There is nothing more sapping of your vitality and spirit than carrying around negativity and bitterness. Don't get me wrong, I am by no means a 'hard' person, strong, yes, but not hard. On the contrary, my emotional state tends to be quite close to the surface.

The break-up of a relationship is sad. The break-up of a relationship that involves children is even sadder, as they can suffer as a result of something over which they have no control. My view is that, as the adults in this, it is up to us to make it the best we can for our children. I have therefore maintained a good relationship with their father and done everything I can to ensure that my children maintain a good relationship with him. I am also delighted that they have a very positive, healthy relationship with his wife and their sister and brother. I could have quite easily have jeopardised that, had I given in to my negative emotions, and thought, spoke and behaved negatively.

Two people I know have demonstrated this positivity in the face of adversity in much more challenging life circumstances; James Taylor, Debbie Clarke and Andrew Davies.

James Taylor was a Nottinghamshire and England cricketer, who described his world as having been turned "upside down" because of a serious, life-threatening heart condition.

At 26-year-old and having been capped 34 times for England James collapsed and was diagnosed with ARVC (arrhythemogenic right ventricular cardiomyopathy), a rare disease of the heart muscle which bears the risk of sudden cardiac arrest. The disease can be controlled with medication or surgery, but not cured. James underwent an operation to have an implantable cardioverter defibrillator fitted which is a battery-powered device under the skin that tracks heart rate and delivers an electric shock to restore a normal heartbeat if it detects an abnormal rhythm.

The condition means that James has had to come to terms with the fact he can no longer play professional sport and live with a life-threatening illness. However, he has remained positive and focused on the future. Even in the first week James wrote on Twitter: *Safe to say this has been the toughest week of my life! My world is upside down. But I'm here to stay and I'm battling on!*

Having the positivity to recognise and seize new opportunities, James has taken on plenty of media work and coaching roles, including working with England U19s and he is relishing both.

'I have always tried to be as positive as I can, and I have kept that way of thinking,' Taylor said. *'I am really happy. Yes, I am not playing cricket and doing what I love, but now I can gradually do a little bit more exercise and am loving the coaching and media work. Coaching is helping people and giving back what I learnt as a player. I want to see what they can achieve and have an impact. I only want to do things I do enjoy but also, most importantly, where I can make a difference to people. I feel I can make a difference with the coaching. I have battled through that moment and most importantly, mentally I am in a good frame of mind. I can't control what's going on physically, but mentally I am in a good space.'*

Debbie Clarke is a friend and fellow business woman, who also founded, and leads, a local network for other business women. Aged 29, a single mum with a one-year old daughter, Debbie was diagnosed with Hodgkins Lymphoma. In a recent blog about this time, one of the things Debbie emphasises the importance of mindset and focusing on the positive:

'Your state of mind makes a big difference
Whatever you face in life, you can choose to smile at it and embrace it or be cross and angry about it. We are all allowed to be cross at bad news at first, but then we need to move on and conquer.

I could have disappeared into myself and spent a lot of time crying (and vomiting – chemo is the worst), but instead I sat back and thought; 'What can I learn from this situation? What positives can come from this? How can I use this to grow and develop? Where are the positives? **You have the power in** *all situations. You can't always change what is happening to you, but you can choose how you deal with it. That is where your power is. Choose positivity. And I'm not saying we have to be positive all the time; that would be insanity. Of course, we all have shit days, but on the whole, once you've picked yourself and your snotty tissues up, choose to look for the bright side.'*

Andrew Davies was diagnosed with a rare form of leukaemia at the age of 13.

'After my diagnosis, my attitude and approach towards life became very simple. I decided from that moment onwards that I would always try and say yes whenever I was given the opportunity to do something. The word yes is one of the most powerful words available to you and in the years since I was ill, that's become very clear to me.'

Aged 14 Andrew decided to raise money for the children's hospital where he was treated and he said, *'I'll raise the cost of my bone marrow transplant treatment'*, without knowing how much that was. When he discovered that was £150,000, he remained undaunted and said, 'yes' to that being his target. Six years on, with numerous small and large fundraising events, Andrew had raised £147,259!

Saying yes, whilst studying for GCSE's and A Levels has led to many great experiences that has included making DVDs, speaking at large events, achieving Gold Duke of Edinburgh Award, sailing with the Ellen MacArthur Cancer Trust, being a participant in 2016 BBC's Children in Need 470mile Rickshaw Challenge and speaking to 5,500 people about the challenge at the Royal Albert Hall.

I've not always maintained my positive mindset, but I'm a learner.
I have made mistakes; I have been, and can be, overly critical: seeing what has not been done rather than focusing on what has been achieved, with myself, at home and at work. These mistakes, and the consequences, have only made me realise how important it is to remain relentlessly positive.

Using a version of the old 'Praise Sandwich' always achieves better results: praising what has been done before suggesting an improvement and then following up with praise; both with ourselves and those around us.

What I have learned is the huge importance of maintaining a positive mental attitude; it is one of the most important factors if we are to live the life we choose.

Laughter is the sun that drives winter from the human face.
Victor Hugo

Affirmations:

- *I am grateful every day for the abundance in my life.*
- *I am feeling the benefits of being positive with myself, and others, and I feel good.*
- *I am being positive about what I can achieve and am achieving more each day.*
- *I am using my 'bubble' to protect myself from negativity.*
- *I am feeling the huge benefits of being much more positive with all those around me.*

 ACTION

Ditch the Soaps

Where can we experience negativity and the worst side of the moaning cycle of negativity on a daily basis? The soaps. They are full of doom and gloom, hopelessness and the nastiness of life (with only the occasional party to lighten the mood). Eliminating soap operas from our lives can have a profound affect on our capacity to be more positive and see the positive side of life. Try it for 21 days, the time it takes to change a habit, see how much more positive you feel.

Watch Your Language

Reflect on the words you use with yourself and those around you:

Watch your **thoughts**, they become words,
Watch your **words**, they become actions,
Watch your **actions**, they become habits,
Watch your **habits**, they become character,
Watch your **character**, it becomes your destiny.

Lao Tze

The activities and tools mentioned below are designed for all ages, and you can adapt as appropriate to try with children and young people.
They are available on www.equipped2succeed.co.uk

Positive Mental Attitude – The Rules for Creating the Habit
Positive Alphabet – on occasions, we all need help finding the right words to reframe in the positive.
Practising Gratitude – a few tools to support an attitude of gratitude

NB: This chapter in no way attempts to deal with issues related to clinical depression or any other related mental health issues, only to provide helpful reflection and a few tools that may be helpful.

Chapter Eight

The Power of Passion

Attaching powerful emotions to our goals

There is no passion to be found playing small – in settling for a life that is less than the one you are capable of living.
Nelson Mandela

passion: *strong and barely controllable emotion;*
an intense desire or enthusiasm for something;
a thing arousing great enthusiasm.

When Billy Elliot (in the film 'Billy Elliot') is asked in his audition what it feels like when he's dancing, he says:
'It's like electricity running through my body'.
That is passion.

The most successful people pursue things they are passionate about. They pursue things to which they attach powerful emotions. This helps maintain their drive and determination, even when the going gets tough. Their enthusiasm is obvious and infectious, helping attract that all-important support that everyone needs to succeed.

Passion is energy. Feel the power that comes from focusing on what excites you.
Oprah Winfrey

Most of us rarely define what we really want, or identify what we're really passionate about, let alone really believe that we can follow our passions. Most of us have dreams and passions as children and young people, but we're often taught to be sensible and realistic, rather than to follow our passions.

Finding our passion is as important as finding out what we're good at. Genetic pre-disposition and technical ability are important to succeed in sports, dancing and many other areas of physical activity, as is a predisposition for Mathematics and Science if we want to pursue Medicine or Engineering. However, it is passion that sets apart those people who train and study harder and longer and give more time, focus and energy. In short, passion gives people the fire to go that extra mile, to pursue excellence, rather than settling for mediocrity. There are many young people with less innate ability who achieve more because their passion gives them the drive to work harder and sacrifice more to achieve their goals. Many have achieved phenomenal success with passion, a phenomenal work ethic and a willingness to learn, rather than obvious technical ability or traditional study and career path. Look at the achievements of Richard Branson, Alan Sugar, Mary Kay Ash and Oprah Winfrey.

Nobel Prize Winners are epitomised by passion in their field, rather than traditional academic excellence being a common denominator, whether that is Nobel Peace prize winner Nadia Murad, striving to eliminate sexual violence as a weapon of war and armed conflict or winner of the Nobel Prize in Physics, Richard Feynman. Many successful people in sport and the arts achieve far greater things than peers with more natural ability because of their unstoppable passion. Look at Sally Gunnell's journey to win gold in the 400 metre hurdles at the Barcelona Olympics in 1992, against all the odds and all the predictions of more 'natural' athletes winning. Read more about Sally's passion and mental approach in the *Develop Your Winning Brain* chapter. We can all think of sports teams and dance groups who, with their passion and enthusiasm, have beaten an opposition that is technically better on paper.

> *Find joy in everything you choose to do.*
> *Every job, relationship, home...*
> *it's your responsibility to love it, or change it.*
> Chuck Palahniuk

Passion is not always what we do, but sometimes we do things to achieve our passion; we follow a path that brings the outcomes we want. Young people don't study for years to become a barrister because they love to study, but rather because of what they can achieve as a barrister. There are people who are passionate about business: the whole process and the rewards it brings. They are not necessarily passionate about the business they are in, but the art of doing business. Of course, combining both takes satisfaction in business achievements to another level. Anita Roddick combined her passion for natural products with a passion for ethical business to found *The Body Shop*. She demonstrated that you can make a profit and make a positive contribution to the community; you can trade on a global scale and support campaigns for human rights, whilst opening scores of shops a year. Reviewing the second edition of her book, *Business as Usual*, the Guardian said: 'There is no disputing Anita Roddick's passion and she has now poured her heart out to help those who want to follow in her footsteps'. Paul Smith has pursued business in his passion, tailored clothing with a twist, with shops in many major capital cities. He started by learning tailoring at night school in Nottingham and, in a recent documentary he demonstrated that same passion and enthusiasm that got him started.

Fun is important in communication, and so is passion. I believe that communication is the most important tool of leadership and passion is the most important element of communication. It is passion, above all, that persuades. For all its modern emphasis on communication, so much of business forgets this crucial element.
Anita Roddick

There are elements of science that are beyond the understanding of many, but there are people who, with their enthusiasm for sharing their passion, bring it to life for us. These include Stephen Hawking, with one of the biggest-selling books on physics of all time: *A Brief History Of Time: From Big Bang To Black Holes* and Susan Greenfield, author of: *The Secret Life of the Brain*, who has done much to help us understand the field of neuroscience with her enthusiastic talks and writing about how the brain works. Richard Feynman, theoretical physicist and a Nobel Prize winner, throughout his career demonstrated his passion and enthusiasm for exploring the world around him. Thanks to You Tube, a new audience is discovering Richard Feynman's talents as a brilliant, inspiring physicist and communicator. One of the biggest hits on YouTube is a new animated video, featuring Richard Feynman's words, which has gone viral. In the film, Feynman can be heard extolling the beauty and wonders of science contained within a simple flower. As well as the flower video, *THE FEYNMAN SERIES (part 1) – Beauty*, which, to date, has been watched nearly three quarters of a million times, there are many other videos featuring his ground-breaking theories which clearly demonstrate his enthusiasm and passion for his work.

 ## So, Why Is Passion So Important?

Powerful, positive emotions give us self-motivation and infectious enthusiasm, the get up and go, to achieve our goals, and passion is one of the most powerful emotions. We will ultimately succeed in the goals we are passionate about.

> *Dreams are astoundingly important.*
> *They keep nagging you because you're supposed to fulfil them.*
> *When you sense you're special, you're not neurotic or grandiose. Something inside you is calling to you and you have to listen. When you love to do something; that means you have a gift for it...*
> *And when you're gifted at something, you have to do it.*
> Barbara Sher

Successful people attach powerful emotions to their goals, and if we want to equip our children to succeed in achieving their dreams and goals, we need to do all we can to empower and enable them to find and pursue their passions. Firstly, we need to allow them to pursue things in which they show an interest (rather than what we want them to be interested in). This may entail trying lots of different things to find those specific things that spark their interest. We then need to do whatever we can to enable our children to pursue those passions.

To Feel It   To Be Enthusiastic   To Be Focused

The road to success is fuelled by determination. For me, there's a simple equation which leads to determination:

$$goals + passion = determination$$

determination: *a decisive, unwavering movement towards reaching a set goal or end.*

Being passionate and enthusiastic about what we do is a huge contributory factor to realising our goals. Passion and enthusiasm also help us to enthuse others, which increases our chances of success.

Enthusiasm Can Make Things 100% Better

I have frequently been accused of being 'too enthusiastic', often by people who see their role as a job, or who have lost their passion, enthusiasm and energy for what they do. I don't think we can be too enthusiastic; it's a matter of focusing our enthusiasm. I have had a long journey to really focus my enthusiasm and there have been times when my enthusiasm has bubbled over in ways that may make people not want to get into lifts with me!

Fall in love with some activity, and do it! Nobody ever figures out what life is all about, and it doesn't matter. Explore the world. Nearly everything is really interesting if you go into it deeply enough. Work as hard and as much as you want to on the things you like to do the best. Don't think about what you want to be, but what you want to do. Keep up some kind of a minimum with other things so that society doesn't stop you from doing anything at all.

Richard P. Feynman

 **My Realisation!**

I can remember exactly when the significance of passion was really brought home to me. After a particularly tough time in my life, challenging personally and in my career, I was considering leaving my field, education, and pursuing another area. I was at a cross roads, and was associating the stresses, strains and negativity I was feeling at the time with the education world in general, rather than just my role at that time. All I could think was that I needed to move away from something about which I cared so deeply. As part of some development work I was leading, outside my main role, I was at a conference in Edinburgh and all I remember about that conference is hearing Jack Black, of Mindstore, speak. He only spoke for a short time, but it was enough. He emphasised the importance of passion if we are to succeed and be where we're meant to be. I leaned over to the person I was with and said: 'Education and learning is the only work I'm passionate about'. I just needed to find where I could best pursue what I believed was important: improving the capacity of people to realise their potential. In short: empowering, enabling and equipping people of any age or situation to realise their dreams and goals and to succeed. Like most key moments in our lives, I remember that moment as if it was yesterday, sitting in that hall and realising that I needed to follow my passion in education and not be defined by the job role I was in. That moment started the journey to this book.

If we know what we're passionate about and believe it's legitimate to pursue that passion, we start channelling it - doing all the things we need to do to achieve our dreams.

I am always expanding my understanding of the power of passion and. I recently enjoyed Sir Ken Robinson's book that explores finding your passions and talents in great depth. *Finding Your Element - How to Discover Your Talents and Passions and Transform Your Life.*

Language and Body Language

Our language and body language communicate our passion, as well as our positivity. There are times when we need to do things that we may not be enthusiastic about: chores for our home, essential caring activities for our family, challenging training sessions and essential work towards our goals. Enthusiasm helps us to do all of those things more joyously and successfully, things such as study, examinations, basic work to earn the money to start our business or save the deposit for our first home, maintain our fitness regime, projects at work or work on our home. If we do everything with enthusiasm, it's far less like hard work. We are also more likely to get support from others, such as teachers, officials, coaches, work colleagues if we do things with enthusiasm. If we are in an interview, seeking support for ourselves or a project or venture, or in any other circumstance where we are in competition with others for a place, role or support, we are much more likely to succeed if we do it with passion and enthusiasm. Passion and enthusiasm are simply invaluable if we are to realise our potential, and reach our goals.

The passionate are the only advocates who always persuade.
The simplest man with passion will be more persuasive
than the most eloquent without.
Rene Descartes

We can change our mindset by altering our language and body language, and vice versa.

Language We Associate With Enthusiasm And Passion:
Yes
I will
I am
I want
Vision
Strength
Absolutely
I'm sure

There's no doubt in my mind

Language we associate with a lack of enthusiasm and passion:
Maybe
We'll see
Not sure
I might if I can
That would be OK but.....
It's all right for her / him but ... (then comes the negative envy or excuse)
I'd do that if I could but .... (then comes the excuse!)
I'd like to do that but I can't see me............
(then comes the low aspiration and lack of self-belief
that become fear of failure and an excuse!)

Body language we associate with enthusiasm and passion:
Smiling
Energetic
Intense

Body language we associate with a lack of enthusiasm and passion:
Slow
Lethargic
Looking bored
'Going through the motions'

Building and Maintaining Passion and Enthusiasm

There are a few things we can do to really develop, maintain and use our passion and enthusiasm to help us realise our goals and ward off that doubting voice in our heads. We need to consciously enthuse, learn and celebrate success to maintain our motivation and to motivate others to help us pursue our goals. These are also things we can do with our children to help them develop their enthusiasm and passion for life and the things they want to achieve.

Find out More – Become an Expert – Become the Best.

To pursue our passions and succeed, we need to be enthusiastic and learn more about the things we are passionate about, e.g. Business, Sport, Medicine, Science, Music, Law, Engineering or Dance. Children and those who succeed in pursuing their passion have a great capacity to focus: to be completely absorbed in one thing to the exclusion of everything else. That's how Bill Gates became an expert in computers. And any successful person will tell you the importance of having that sort of focus.

Show Enthusiasm in Everything We Do

Liven up our smiles, not with that false, painted-on smile, but honest smiling with our eyes, as well as our mouth. Think about how you smile when you greet people. Show your appreciation through your smile. Communicate your passion, enthusiasm and energy through your body language. We all need to get on well with people, personally, socially, and in our work. Smiling, enthusing and taking an interest in others is an essential starting point. We also need the help of others to achieve our goals. Enthusiasm is infectious.

Broadcast Good News – Celebrate Success

Share good news with friends, family, and people you work with. This is not bragging or boasting; it's sharing positive, good news. Don't be like the energy sappers, mood hoovers and tabloid newspapers: focused on the negative. Broadcasting good news activates you, makes you feel better, and makes others feel better, too.

I have a passion and enthusiasm for life, for the small things, as well as the bigger things, and have endeavoured to keep that awe and wonder which we all have when we're young to fuel my continued passion for pursuing what's important to me.

Affirmations:

- *I am passionately enjoying what I do.*
- *I am passionate about achieving ……………...*
- *I am passionately learning everything I need to …….*
- *I am passionately making the most of opportunities.*

 ACTION

Persist
Advance
Strong
Strive
Integrity
Optimism
Nothing interferes

To achieve your goal, your life may sound like a perfume counter: full of Passion and Obsession, leading to Joy. Do It!

It's therefore important to imagine ourselves experiencing the things we're passionate about, and bringing our imagination to life: seeing what we want to achieve in bright, vibrant technicolour: hearing it, smelling it, tasting it. Using all of our senses to bring our passion to life in our imagination.

To help bring things to life and fuel our imagination, it can be helpful to create a visual collage of what realising our passion looks like: images that help us clearly picture the desired outcomes of passion. We can do this as a poster or electronically, whichever works best for us.

Fuel Your Passion

Below are some prompts to help you reflect on your passions. You can use these yourself and, adapted appropriately for their age, with your children.

1. When do you feel passionate?
   How do you feel when you are passionate about something?
   What is it about those times or that activity that makes you feel like that?

2. What do you do that you feel passionate about?
   daily
   weekly
   monthly
   annually

3. It's important to set a goal to ensure we think about and DO the things we are passionate about more often - at least some part of every day, or, if it's something from which we want to earn our living, we need to wholeheartedly pursue our passion.

Every artist was first an amateur.
Ralph Waldo Emerson

Here is some food for thought that you can also adapt to use with your children, your colleagues or your clients:

If you are passionate about getting a 'good' job and earning 'good' money (only you can define good for you!) find out about the sort of work you like; spend time imagining yourself in that role, read about that work, study, take courses and find opportunities to get experience in the sort of work you like.

If you are passionate about having your own business, spend time imagining yourself in business and find information, read about those who have started their own business, get advice (there's lots of free advice out there) develop your skills and find ways to get experience in the sort of business you would like.

If one of your passions is a particular sport or athletic pursuit, set a goal, join a club or join a better club, get a coach, talk to people in that sport, plan in enough time to practise, play, watch or read about those who have reached the pinnacle in your sport.

If one of your passions is films: set a goal and plan going to the cinema every week, two weeks, month to suit your circumstances. Find out what's on and find someone who would like to go with you (don't drag along a reluctant friend as it will only spoil your enjoyment, and this is about **your** passions).

If your passion is to make a film, make one, it doesn't matter how amateur to start with. You will only learn properly about film making by doing it. 'You Tube' has made it easier; any of us can now make a film.

If you are passionate about travel; spend time imagining yourself in the places you want to travel to; find information and ways to visit, work in, and experience the places you want to travel to.

> *Life is not a mystery to be contemplated.*
> *It is an adventure to be chartered.*
> *Create your destiny!*
> Kristen Goodsell

Those who clearly know what they want, are passionate about achieving it; and are prepared to do what it takes, in energy, time and effort, are the exception. They are fuelled to succeed.

Chapter Nine

Vision – Goals – Action

Creating Your Own Future History

*The greater danger for most of us lies not in setting our aim too
high and falling short: but in setting our aim too low,
and achieving our mark.*
Michelangelo

vision: *the faculty or state of being able to see;
the ability to think about or plan the future with imagination or
wisdom;
a mental image of what the future will or could be like.*

goal: *the object of a person's ambition or effort; an aim or desired
result;
the result or achievement toward which effort is directed; aim;
the destination of a journey.*

All successful people:
- dream and think big;
- have goals;
- believe they will achieve their goals;
- plan and work purposefully, step by step,
- to realise their goals;
- use their imagination to really see, feel and hear
- themselves achieving their dreams.

*Champions aren't made in the gyms. Champions are made
from something they have deep inside them –
a desire, a dream, a vision.*
Muhammad Ali, Heavyweight Boxing Champion

We all have dreams, but how many of us believe our dreams are attainable? How many of us turn those dreams into goals and really see ourselves achieving them? Dreams that we convince ourselves are unobtainable are much safer than specific goals and action plans that we can measure ourselves against. Leaving them as dreams means we don't have to risk failure.

All successful people map their path to achieving their dreams – one step at a time, or take huge leaps of faith when an opportunity arises. There are those in every field who have enormous natural ability, instinct, and the winning mentality to succeed, and we can all learn from them. They DO THE WORK: systematically set goals, map out the steps, and deliberately put one foot in front of the other each day towards achieving their goals using every opportunity that arises.

Goals give us deliberate, conscious focus on what we want to
BE – DO – HAVE
and enable us to spot those all important opportunities to realise them.

Setting goals is all about deciding what we really want, and using our imagination and positive thinking to enable us to see, hear and feel ourselves realising our dreams and goals. As Muhammad Ali put it: 'create your own future history'. An important part of systematically setting goals is writing them down. We then need to start mapping the steps and taking deliberate action every day. This enables us to attract and spot the right opportunities, as well as engaging support from appropriate people to achieve our goals and create our own positive future.

Decide the destination – create the map – move round obstacles – take the shortest route around detours – keep the momentum moving forward towards our destination.

One thing that's really important in setting goals is to **focus on what we want to BE – DO – HAVE...**not on what we don't want. All too often, we're clear about what we *don't* want, but a bit hazy about what we really *do* want. To paraphrase Shirley McLaine, dwelling on what we don't want adds to its power. Likewise, *dwelling on what we do want adds to its power.*

We need to ensure we focus our thinking and energies on what we really want!

 Setting goals and taking action to achieve them helps us to use our thinking, time, energy and effort on realising our own positive future.

I really wish I'd learned the power of setting goals earlier in life. Not the narrow targets you are set by other people at school or in work, but life goals. I realise I have naturally had goals from a very young age. However, had I learned the process and techniques described in this chapter, I feel I could have wasted less time, achieved more in life and work, been myself more and had more fun!

There is a great deal of evidence in all human endeavour that demonstrates the power of setting goals. Don't get me wrong, setting goals is not the whole answer to achieving those big dreams; it's just the start, the guiding thread that keeps us focused on the path ahead and helps put set-backs into perspective. Specific, measurable goals help us make decisions, drive us forward in the right direction and enable us to maintain the passion, enthusiasm, energy, vitality and perseverance necessary to realise our dreams.

A person who aims at nothing is sure to hit it.
Anonymous

Successful people know where they want to get to; although they rarely know exactly *how* they are going to get there, the 'how' 'comes'. Most very successful people naturally dream and think big, and they use the power of their imagination to believe and see themselves achieving their dreams, keeping themselves focused on the 'prize', which is especially useful when the going gets tough. Everyone has doubt. Everyone has moments of, 'Can I really do this?' Having very clear goals, and seeing and feeling ourselves achieving them, helps us silence the negative 'chimp' in our head. Dr Steve Peters' brilliant book: *The Chimp Paradox* expertly explains how we can stop ourselves from sabotaging our own success by taking control of our negative 'chimp'. With clear goals, plans and belief we can counter-balance negative thoughts and emotions and silence the doubting voice in our head: the voice that gives us excuses not to do things and persuades us that what we really want is not attainable.

So What Stops Us from Focusing On Our Dream and Setting Big Goals?

There are people who put their dreams in a little box and say,
'Yes, I've got dreams, of course I've got dreams.'
Then they put the box away and bring it out once in awhile to look in it, and yep, they're still there.
These are great dreams, but they never even get out of the box.
It takes an uncommon amount of guts to put your dreams on the line, to hold them up and say, 'How good or how bad am I?'
That's where courage comes in.'
Erma Louise Bombeck

Many of us are frightened to dream and think big, and we talk ourselves out of even daring to dream about what we really want. Our thinking is dominated by doubt, and many of us have been brought up in an environment that keeps our thinking small. How many times have you been told to 'be realistic'; has this prevented you from doing something? We are too often overly influenced by the prevailing attitude and aspiration within our immediate environment and wider community; limited in our dreams by the attitude, *'people like us don't do things like that'*.

If you accept the expectations of others, especially negative ones, then you will never change the outcome.
Michael Jordan

It has taken me years to have the courage and faith to develop, deliver programmes, and write equipped2succeed. I have always sought more credibility and experience to counter balance the doubt. 'Being realistic' is the line given to us by those who are happy to keep the bar low, and it can mean that our dreams are not nurtured, but starved of the positive energy they need.

Be realistic is the most commonly travelled road to mediocrity.
Why would you be realistic? What's the point of being
realistic? It's unrealistic to walk into a room and flick a switch
and lights come on. That's unrealistic.
Fortunately Edison (and others) didn't think so.
Will Smith

Most of us are paralysed by thinking that we need to know 'how' before we start. However, what we need to do is start by defining exactly what we want to achieve: specifically what we want to do, have or be. What we need to do is to get started. Define what we really want to achieve and this will fuel our brains to go to work, generating ideas and spotting opportunities for us to create the path to our dreams.

It has been proven that people who set goals achieve success. Consistently working with our goals enables us to obtain the results we seek. Successful people set goals and truly believe they are going to achieve them. They then focus their thinking, talents, energy and internal resources on realising their goals.

Empowering Ourselves (and those around us) Means
Being a Dream-Maker, not a Dream-Stealer.

DREAM AND THINK BIG!

The reason most people never reach their goals is that they
don't define them, learn about them, or ever seriously consider
them as believable or achievable.
Winners can tell you where they are going,
what they plan to do along the way,
and who will be sharing the adventure with them.
Denis Waitley

So why is it that we are not systematically taught the power of setting goals and how to set them in school? I don't know, but I really hope I can contribute to addressing that gap. Not the narrow targets set by others: teachers, parents or, when we're older, managers in work, but life goals. Children naturally have dreams and goals, but all too often they are dampened by that dream-stealing phrase 'be realistic'.

Determination, persistence and perseverance come from having goals, aiming for something we really want.

Setting goals and doing what is necessary to achieve them is a habit, and the sooner we develop that habit, the easier it is for us to start achieving the things we really want in life.

 # Setting Goals

Create a Vision

Take up one idea. Make that one idea your life – think of it, dream of it, live on that idea. Let the brain, muscles, nerves, every part of your body, be full of that idea, and just leave every other idea alone. This is the way to success.
Swami Vivekananda

The first step to creating our own future is to have a vision of the future we want and then set goals to achieve it.

Muhammad Ali is credited with using the phrase: 'Create your own future history'. What he meant was: set goals, see, hear and feel ourselves achieving our goals, believe, and do the work. This enables us to focus and it also helps us to overcome challenges and barriers, and to remain persistent and resilient.

To create our vision and goals, we need time without agenda, schedule, 'to do' lists or commitments to allow our mind to use its infinite power. Our visions are unique to us: no one can see ours and we can't see anyone else's, even our sister's, partner's or children's. We can create our vision in all sorts of ways and some people find vision boards very powerful, predominantly using images rather than words. It's also essential top share our vision, if we are to support, enable and empower each other to achieve our respective visions, but we can't own others' visions.

If you can DREAM it, you can DO it.
All of our dreams can come true – if we have the
courage to pursue them.
Walt Disney

Your vision leads to specific goals.
We then need to continuously and consistently see, hear, and feel ourselves realising our vision and goals.
The other ingredient, of course, is disciplined, deliberate action – moving forward every day.

Translating Dreams into Specific Goals and Action

For me, Joel A. Baker, simply summarises the power of combining vision and action:

Vision without action is merely a dream.
Action without vision just passes the time.
Vision with action can change the world.

The process outlined below is all about translating what you want to do, your dreams and ideas, into your future reality. This is a systematic goal-setting process, with specific information about what you may do at each stage. It's a time-intensive process to start with, but like everything, the more you do it, the easier it becomes. You will make the process your own and adapt it to suit you and those around you.

Goal-Setting Process

Summary of the Steps

Step 1 **Make an 'I want list'**
Things you want to **BE – DO – HAVE.**

Step 2 Choose a few things from your 'I want list' to translate into **specific GOALS and ACTION PLANS.**

Step 3 **Create your goals.**

Step 4 **Create reminders of your GOALS.**

Step 5 **Create action plans for each of your GOALS.**

Step 6 **TAKE ACTION: keep moving forward towards your goals.**
Stay in the now and take one step at a time.

Step 7 **BELIEVE**
Visualise and mentally rehearse. See, feel and hear yourself achieving your GOALS.
When you face set-backs, keep your eye on the prize...YOUR GOAL.

Step 8 **REVIEW REVIEW REVIEW**
Where do I want to be?
Where am I now?
What are the next steps?
Who can help me?
What am I going to do about it?

The steps detailed below share the process, and the rationale behind it. Once we know what to do, it becomes a simple process.

The challenging bit is the discipline and focus of doing what we need to do each day. However, that becomes so much easier if our goals are aligned with our interests, passions, and what we're good at.

Step 1   Make an 'I want list' – Things you Want to BE – DO – HAVE.

I do this myself every time I do a goal-setting workshop, and there's always something new in what I write down that surfaces from my sub-conscious.

It helps to have some quiet, relaxing music on, without the distraction of lyrics. My favourite are some Ludovico Einaudi tracks. There are many suitable tracks on the eqquipped2succeed playlists.

Give yourself 15 minutes and make a list of everything you want to BE, HAVE, DO. Have a piece of paper with columns for each one, if it helps. There's sometimes a crossover between them, but that's OK. You're just trying to still your mind and focus on what you really want. There are overlaps in these 3 areas but that doesn't matter. It's about your reflecting on what you really want to:

BE – the sort of person you want to be, e.g. positive, passionate, enthusiastic, caring, tolerant, kind, assertive, focused and valuing every day.

DO – the things you want to do: for example; develop a new form of ….., grow a business, work for myself, contribute in my community, write, play ….. a particular sport, play a …. musical instrument, make a record, travel to …., set up a ….. charity / community organisation.

HAVE – the things you want to have: for example a career I enjoy, a family, a successful business, a house or a particular type of house, in a particular place, a mortgage-free house, a particular type of car, a particular award or qualification.

Step 2 Choose a few things from your '**I want list**' to translate into **specific GOALS and ACTION PLANS.**

Please make sure you have just a few goals and avoid overload: you can't focus on umpteen things at once, which I've discovered to my cost. Too often, I have spread myself too thinly, which has resulted in the frustration of only partly achieving my main goals. I recommend no more than two or three big goals, with two of three on-going personal development or 'maintenance' goals. Some will be big dreams and will take a while to realise, some will be more obtainable ones, that contribute to your big goals. You may want to start your own business and alongside that develop your positive mental attitude. In your personal development, you may focus on one area of the twelve elements of the equipped2succeed framework each month. Maintenance goals are vital so that, whilst we're pursuing our big goals, we don't lose sight of the importance of those things we need to do constantly and consistently, like maintain our health and energy, and spend quality time with our family.

Look at the Wheel of Life categories in Chapter two; *What is Success?*, which helps us decide our current and longer-term priorities. These will be a combination of working towards bigger goals and maintenance goals. I recommend most people to think about creating and maintaining balance in their lives and choosing goals in different areas of life. However, sometimes it's relevant to focus on one; for example; for those who want to be elite athletes, or for those seeking to move on from challenging times personally, financially or in any other way, it is essential to focus on the main goal and then other things we want to BE – DO – HAVE, will stem from that. For example, this morning I watched a news article on Australian TV about a 10year old girl who'd lost 30 kilos in the last year. Her mother had decided to take things in hand and find a way for her daughter to lose weight. With some tenacity and perseverance, and trying all sorts of things, they had eventually walked 4 miles 3 times a week to help achieve the weight loss. By focusing on that, other benefits had flowed: the bullying and teasing about weight had stopped, self-esteem had, in the mother's words, 'sky rocketed', the girl was now on sports teams and was generally enjoying life much more.

The other important factor is that need to create medium-term goals and current, specific goals and actions that are steps along the way to reaching our big goals.

Maintenance Goals – Establishing Positive Habits

Some goals are what I call maintenance goals. They are things we want to develop as on-going positive habits such as a regular pattern of exercise, or healthy diet, and spending quality time doing something with our loved ones. We may need to focus on these at a specific time, to create positive habits. Once we've established these habits, we pursue them as a day-to-day discipline and they no longer need to be a focus of our goals. For example, I had a goal many years ago to ensure that I had focused, quality time with my children, not just the things we all need to do on a day-to-day basis. I was working long hours, they were growing up and I believe you need to devote as much, if not more, high-quality time with your children when they're older than when they're very young. Their needs are different when they get to the latter stages of primary school and as they enter their early teens. This is often a more challenging time, but that's when you need to do the work to ensure you reframe and reinforce the values you endeavoured to establish when they were younger.

This goal focused me and ensured that important, urgent work didn't take priority all the time. I ensured my children didn't miss things that were important to them which mainly revolved around sports: training, practices, and competitions or matches. I could easily have found excuses to occasionally not take them, my work, their school work, being a lone parent, but that would have been abdicating my responsibility, and certainly not in line with my vision. I would leave work to make sure they got there they needed to be, and this also reinforced with them the importance of commitment. My car certainly 'knew its own way' to many local sporting venues. I only needed to set this goal once and the pattern became established, which meant I achieved my goal of enabling my children to pursue their dreams and passions and we spent a lot of time talking whilst we travelled.

Maintenance goals could include things like:

- Developing a positive mental attitude and consistently using positive language.
- Being D.E.A.R. to ourselves:
  Maintaining:
  - a healthy **D**iet
  - an **E**xercise regime – finding a regime that suits you and doing it!
  - a positive **A**ttitude
  - a pattern of high quality **R**est
- Consistently making time for our loved ones.
- **Consistently sticking to our plan: doing what we say we're going to do when we say we're going to do it!** Using our dairying or TO DO lists and not making excuses for ourselves.

Step 3 **Create Your Goals**

I have developed a number of goal-setting templates for different ages, and a selection are available as downloads on www.equipped2succeed.co.uk. The essential ingredients of setting a goal for me are:

GOAL - Be specific and make it measurable.

What's in it for me? What are the specific benefits from achieving my goal? How will I feel?

What's in it for others? I believe that every worthwhile goal has benefit for others. Whether that's being a role model for younger family members, or being able to financially support my family.

Vision: It's vital that you can see yourself achieving your goal, and know what it looks and feels like. Having a visual stimulus that encapsulates your goal helps you do this: for example a photo of the 'prize', a house, a business, a trophy or medal, a certificate, yourself smiling back at you with your goal realised.

Affirmations: An affirmation is a personal, positive thought or statement in the first person, present tense, affirming that your desired goal has been reached, or is within reach.

Create a few affirmations as if you've already achieved your goal and make sure they are dynamic and full of positive feelings: for example;

I am enjoying training to be a ……..
I am loving the freedom and joy I feel in the water now I can swim.
I am excitedly reading my results which are …….
I am loving the stimulation of studying at my chosen university.
I am proudly sharing my leadership qualification.
I am loving the feeling of being in our fabulous family home.
I am proudly leading a successful business.

Step 4   Create Reminders of Your GOALS

Create cue cards (credit card sized cards) with your Goal and Affirmation on. Carry your cue cards around with you as a permanent reminder, physically and electronically

Put your goals somewhere prominent where you can look at them every day. Keep them electronically on your phone and computer and read them preferably just before you go to sleep, so that your subconscious can go to work on them whilst you sleep.

Step 5   Create Action Plans for Your GOALS

Big dreams and goals can seem overwhelming until we break them down into bite-sized chunks, and move forward one step at a time (or, for those of us who find it impossible to work on one thing at once, a few steps at a time!) On the equipped2succeed website, there are sample action plan templates. Tailor them to suit you, without losing the essential elements.

What are the next steps you're going to take to achieve your goals? Our action plans should be dynamic. Whilst we need to be focused and disciplined when implementing our plans; but we also need to be adaptable. One road may be closed, or there may be a new road, and just like our satnav, we need to respond appropriately to new situations and opportunities; adjusting and amending plans and road maps as we move forward and reviewing each milestone along the way.

Step 6   **TAKE ACTION** – Keep moving forward towards your goals. Stay in the now and take one step at a time.

DO THE WORK

STAY FOCUSED

STAY DISCIPLINED

SPOT OPPORTUNITIES AND TAKE THEM

Most people live and die with their music still un-played.
They never dare to try.
Mary Kay Ash

Step 7   **BELIEVE IN YOURSELF and YOUR GOAL**

See, feel and hear yourself achieving your GOALS. When you face set backs, keep your eye on the prize...**YOUR GOAL.**

Imagine yourself achieving your goals every day.

I learn from the past but I dream of the future because that is
where I choose to spend the rest of my life.
Humphrey Walters

Relaxation – Visualisation – Mental Rehearsal Process (R – V – MR)

By systematically relaxing, visualising and mentally rehearsing we improve our focus, self-belief and positive thinking to achieve our goals. We can also use our imagination to tap into our brainpower and find solutions to challenges. As you will have read in Chapter six; *Use Your Amazing Winning Brain*, your subconscious mind doesn't know the difference between imagination and reality. We attract what we think about, and using this process helps us spot the opportunities and people who will help us realise our goals. Your subconscious mind believes what you tell it, positive or negative. So, focusing our mind on seeing ourselves achieving our dreams and goals helps us to achieve them. We can also use it to improve our skills and performance in anything we do.

Relax: Enable your mind to be quiet and focused – relaxation will relieve stress, tension and anxiety, allowing your brain to make the right connections to maximize your potential. Let your mind flow.

Visualise Creatively: In your mind, imagine how you want things to be: go on a mental journey, vividly using the power of your creative thinking.

Mentally rehearse achieving your goals: Picture exactly what you want to BE, DO or HAVE; practice scenarios and situations in your head and watch them happen, again and again, like action replays, so you create, choose and take control with the power of your mind.

A full description of the Relaxation – Visualisation – Mental Rehearsal process is in Chapter six; *Use Your Amazing Winning Brain.*

Step 8   REVIEW REVIEW REVIEW

Where do I want to be?
Where am I now?
What are the next steps?
Who can help me?
What am I going to do about it?

Give yourself something to work toward - constantly.
Mary Kay Ash

Like anything else, unless you systematically set goals, take action to achieve them and review where you are, you'll lose momentum and it will become that much harder to achieve your chosen future. Decide what you want to achieve every day; that will take you a few steps closer to achieving your goals. Your goals may change, so recognise when your heart and belief isn't in something and take action to change direction. Don't change just because the going gets tough, only when there's something else that you realise you are more passionate about and have more belief in.

Only those who will risk going too far can possibly find out how far they can go.'
T. S. Eliot

Affirmations

These are general affirmations that we can use, and adapt to make specific for our goals.

- *I am enthusiastically becoming who I want to be.*
- *I am excitedly pursuing my dreams and goals.*
- *I am strong and disciplined to do all the things I need to do to achieve my goals.*
- *I am positively and passionately doing what I need to do to achieve my goals.*

 **ACTION**

Now it's down to you. No one else can do this for you.
No one else will do this for you.

Goal Setting tools on the equipped2succeed website:

Goal Setting Process
Make an 'I want' list
Goal Setting Guidance
Affirmations Guidance
Goal Setting Templates
Goal Action Plan Templates
e2s Relaxation, Visualisation and Mental Rehearsal Tracks

Follow the goal setting process, and use the relaxation, visualisation and mental rehearsal link to support you in achieving your goals and helping those around you set and achieve their goals.

Chapter Ten

Always Learning

Developing Your Growth Mindset

I never cut class. I loved getting A's, I liked being smart.
I liked being on time. I thought being smart is cooler
than anything in the world.
Michelle Obama

learn: *to acquire knowledge of, or skill in, by study, instruction, or experience;*
to gain (a habit, mannerism, etc.) by experience, exposure to example, or the like; acquire;
to start to understand how we must change the way we behave.
always: *at all times; invariably; at any time; in any event.*

Why it is so important to continuously learn

People who thrive are always learning. They are open-minded and have a growth mindset. They are hungry to learn. They expand their comfort zone. They are not the people always moaning about what's wrong without coming up with solutions. We've all met them; they know what's wrong with the country, the local football team, the town, the organisation, other people, and rarely come up with solutions. If they do suggest a solution, it is usually simplistic and/or negative. The moaners rarely learn, improve and grow or succeed.

Those who achieve and succeed are always seeking to grow: expand their understanding and learning; become experts in their field, and
explore horizons beyond. They are hungry to learn, finding sources

of learning and people with experience and expertise in their field from whom they can learn. If you talk to, listen to or read about anyone who is a leader in their field, they will always mention what they have learned from making the most of opportunities, from experience, and from others.

> *Results! Why, man I have gotten a lot of results.*
> *I know several thousand things that won't work.*
> *I am not discouraged because every wrong attempt discarded*
> *is another step forward.*
> Thomas Edison

 Develop a Growth Mindset

> *The person who views the world at fifty the same as he did at*
> *twenty has wasted thirty years of his life.*
> Muhammad Ali

Mindset is a simple idea identified by world-renowned Stanford University psychologist Carol Dweck in decades of research on achievement and success: a simple idea that makes all the difference. '*In a growth mindset, people believe that their most basic abilities can be developed through dedication and hard work – brains and talent are just the starting point. This view creates a love of learning and a resilience that is essential for great accomplishment. Virtually all great people have had these qualities.*' Mindsetonline.com

Successful people find and implement solutions: not just in the obvious fields of science, engineering, technology and business, but in all fields. Look at the way Sir David Brailsford took Great Britain from languishing somewhere near the bottom of world rankings, with two bronze medals at the 1996 Olympics, to one of the most successful cycling nations in the world. Team GB won fourteen cycling medals in Beijing in 2008 (eight gold, four silver and two bronze) and twelve at London 2012 with, again, eight gold. His growth mindset was an essential element of his capacity to lead this phenomenal improvement: challenging the way things were done, identifying issues, finding solutions and implementing change.

C.A.N.I. – Continuous And Never-ending Improvement

To achieve success, we need to be open-minded and learn from everything, not only formal learning. We need to learn from experiences, from others, from our successes, and from our mistakes and failures. It is very powerful if we can view failure or mistakes as a learning opportunity rather than something about which to be ashamed.

Intelligence is the ability to adapt to change.
Steven Hawking

 # Models of Learning

To learn at our best, it's helpful to know something about the learning process. There are a few learning models that help us conceptualise the process of learning and help us focus on what's important. They also emphasise that it's not only about skills and knowledge.

Cycle of Self-Development

There are four distinct aspects of development:

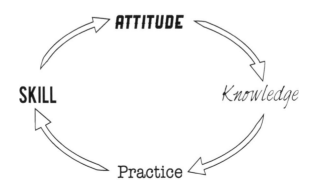

Attitude

It was character that got us out of bed, commitment that moved us into action, and discipline that enabled us to follow through.
Zig Ziglar

The three essential elements of attitude in learning are **need to, want to and can do**. It's important to know and accept what we need to learn, then it's important to really want to learn. The other vital aspect is approaching learning with a can-do attitude. It is often said that our **attitude** determines our **altitude** in life.

Knowledge
Knowledge is essential if we're going to excel. We gain knowledge in all sorts of ways: **formally,** in a school or college, or **informally**. Informal learning is all around us, all the time, if we take notice. This includes:
- listening to those around us and listening to those who have achieved;
- watching others, in person and with the plethora of visual communication we have at our disposal;
- learning from other peoples' experiences and stories;
- modelling the behavior of those who achieve.

Practice
Practice is the **action** part of the process. We only embed learning and develop skills and behaviours with deliberate practice. We have to do the work. It's only by focused, deliberate practice that we become proficient and skilled.

Skill
As time passes, with practice, we become more and more skilled and reach unconscious competence: being able to do something without consciously thinking about it.

Attitude, knowledge, practice, skill provides the basis of a never-ending cycle of continuous improvement.

The K.A.S.H. Box

Another way of looking at learning is the K.A.S.H. box. Some years ago, David Herdlinger reconstructed KSA (Knowlegde, Skill, Attitude) into a quadrant, adding Habits. This has become known as the **K.A.S.H. Box**. The purpose of this was to show that, more often than not, performance, whether individually or organisationally, is not an issue of knowledge and skills, but rather attitudes and habits.

Bringing habits in is interesting, as we all have them, but tend to only notice them in others when they are negative. Positive habits are a crucial element of learning; in our attitude to learning, in the learning process and in ensuring that we embed the things we've learned that are useful to us.

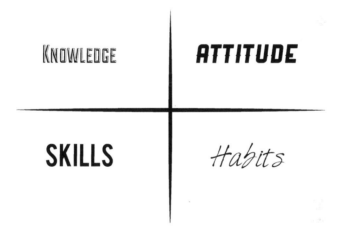

Most people, educational institutions and training organisations spend their energies, both in time and money, on developing the left half of the K.A.S.H Box, Knowledge and Skills.

However, much of the reason for excellent or poor performance in learning, work, sports and all other endeavours is as a result of the right half of the K.A.S.H. Box, Attitude and Habits!

First we make our habits, then our habits make us.
Charles C Noble

Stages of Learning

The more that you read, the more things you will know.
The more that you learn, the more places you'll go.
Dr. Seuss

The following stages of learning are relevant in all the things we need to learn: to live and become the best we can be in our chosen fields. They are as relevant for learning to ride a bike as driving a car, for learning to write as learning to manage relationships.

Unconscious Incompetence

⇩

Conscious Incompetence

⇩

Conscious Competence

⇩

Unconscious Competence

Unconscious Incompetence: This is where we don't know what we don't know. I think this can also relate to people who are not prepared to learn.

Conscious Incompetence: This is when we realise there's something we don't know or a skill we don't have.

Conscious Competence: We have developed knowledge or skill but have to concentrate and deliberately apply ourselves to do it.

Unconscious Competence: Doing things unconsciously:
　'I can do this without even thinking about it.'
　'I have the knowledge and experience to know exactly how to handle this.'
　'It's like riding a bike.'

These stages of learning come to life if we think about all the things we can do without thinking, or from vast experience, that at some point we had to deliberately learn, like riding a bike, writing, managing tasks or situations or using a new computer programme.

 # How We Learn

Tell me, I'll forget. Show me, I'll remember;
Involve me, I'll understand.
Chinese Proverb

To optimise our learning it's helpful (and I would say vital) to understand how we learn.

V.A.K. Learning Styles

The original V.A.K. concepts were first developed by psychologists and teaching specialists starting in the 1920's. V.A.K. theory is valued because its principles and benefits extend to all types of learning and development. I have found the understanding that goes with appreciating that we all learn differently to be useful in enabling individuals to learn more effectively, and to improve communication between colleagues in businesses and organisations.

V – visual – sight

A – audio – hearing

K – kinaesthetic – doing / feeling

Research has shown that three of the five senses prevail when it comes to storing information in the brain. These are visual, through seeing; auditory, through hearing, and kinaesthetic, through physical involvement or doing. We use all of our senses to learn, but most of us find it easier to take in information predominantly through one of these senses. I am used to ensuring workshops cater for the needs of different learners but, on many occasions, I have needed to adapt my preferred communication style to bring out the best in colleagues; such as walking whilst mentoring and talking through things I've emailed. If we have a growth mindset, understand how best we learn, and are aware of different learning styles in others, we are in a much better position to make the most of our potential, and help others to make the most of their potential.

Consider, for a moment, being lost. If you stopped to ask someone how to get to your destination, how would you best remember the information they gave you?

a)   if they just verbally gave you instructions;
b)   if they drew a map for you;
c)   if they either went with you, or described where to go by mentioning some key places with which you could relate, such as a cafe, a shop, or other landmarks.

You will probably find that one or two of these ways works better than the others, and the same is true for all those with whom we communicate.

We all have preferred learning styles, or ways we learn best. There are many ways, in learning and development, of checking our learning style, both in education and in organisations. I have chosen to highlight the V.A.K. learning styles model, as, from my experience, it is a simple way of helping individuals make the most of learning opportunities, helping us all communicate more effectively.

Visual

There are those of us who learn best by seeing things. If we are visual, we prefer to take on board information through sight. There are certain traits that people who are predominantly visual learners share. They may remember faces better than names, or recognise places but have difficulty recalling the street names. They normally talk quite quickly because they are picturing things in their head as they speak. They usually have a good imagination and find it easy to visualise.

Auditory

Some people take in information and learn best through listening. These learners tend to have an advantage in most education systems, where a lecturing mode of instruction often predominates. If people are auditory, they often trust what they hear. If they doubt what is being said, they will want to discuss it. They often talk a lot and sometimes forget that others need to talk, too. This can be a bonus at a party, but not always in a group discussion in training and at work. They find it easier to take and give verbal instructions, and can learn effectively without taking notes because they can easily remember what has been said. They often enjoy background noise when working and like to listen to music or have discussions, and may often talk or hum to themselves.

Kinaesthetic

There are many people who learn best by doing. Kinaesthetic people feel emotions very easily and often become emotionally involved in films, books and events, whether they are happy, scary or sad. Their brain needs time to process information because they are tapping into emotions, relating events to previous experience. This means that they usually talk more slowly and can easily be interrupted by visual learners. Predominantly, kinaesthetic learners have a great memory and can often remember events from early in their childhood. They like to get stuck into a new task rather than be told or shown how to do it. Their surroundings and clothes have to feel comfortable and warm and they often like to stretch out and make themselves comfortable wherever they are.

 This is about empowering us to be the best learners and communicators we can be, rather than using it as an excuse for not taking on board information if it is not presented to us in a way that best suits us.

Just think about the potential impact this has in communication in everyday life. Think about how this may impact on the way we communicate and receive communication from others at home, at work, in social, educational, coaching and training environments.

Reflect on:
- how this may affect the way you communicate in various situations;
- how this may help you interpret others' communication;
- how this may help you learn more effectively;
- how you may help others to communicate and learn more effectively.

We all learn in a combination of ways, and those with higher-order learning skills have developed ways to learn and communicate in all modes, adapting no matter how learning is presented to suit them. When checking preferred learning styles, for example by completing a V.A.K. questionnaire, some people have close scores for all three, and that can indicate that they are able to process information in all three modes: a very strong learning style. For example, whenever I do a learning styles questionnaire, my learning preferences are fairly even, (there is little surprise in that, given my passion for, and experience in, learning), but there is no doubt that my preferred learning style is predominantly visual. I have always made copious notes, both in school and work environments, and find it very difficult to concentrate when someone is talking in work situations unless I have a pen and make notes or doodle. I have very elaborate doodles around my notes during long telephone conversations!

Ways to increase our learning power and improve communication:

If you are predominantly a VISUAL Learner ...
- Write down information.
- Use coloured pens and coloured, unlined paper.
- Use spider charts or mind maps to remember large amounts of information.
- Make mental videos of the facts you need to know.
- Stick post-it notes around to help you remember things.
- Illustrate things with pictures and/or diagrams.
- Use visual prompts to help you remember when presenting.
- Use association techniques e.g. my acronym for remembering how we maximise energy, Being D.E.A.R to

yourself: Diet Exercise Attitude Rest
- Watch a demonstration or video on how to do something before starting.
- Highlight important information in books and notes.

If you are predominantly an AUDITORY learner...
- Repeat things in your head over and over to remember it.
- Take part in discussion.
- Ask to help you clarify and understand.
- Record information you find difficult and listen to it.
- Have background music on while you study or work.
- Discuss what you are going to do with people who can help.
- Have someone ask you questions if you are studying for a test or exam;
- LISTEN well and you will need fewer notes.

If you are predominantly a KINAESTHETIC learner....
- Be comfortable when working.
- Break up times when you need to concentrate every 15 to 20 minutes and move around.
- Volunteer for demonstrations and role-play.
- Walk around as you memorise new information or prepare for anything.
- Play with quiet items, such as Blu-Tack (or similar soft, pliable material), whilst listening to people, studying or thinking.
- Develop good note-taking skills.
- Use mindmaps and other less conventional forms of note-taking.
- Roll up your sleeves and get involved; kinaesthetic people learn from being involved.
- Put information on post-it notes to allow you to manoeuvre it about until it makes sense.

These tips help us to learn more effectively. They also help us get on better with people as we come to understand more about how we all learn and communicate differently.

 Being in the Flow

The quality of a successful person is to flow and not to freeze.
Ralph W. Emerson

Having looked at learning styles, it's worth having a look at the circumstances in which we are likely to learn and work best: when we're in flow. This is not a passive activity, such as being absorbed in a book, but actually using our mind and/or body in an activity that demands our full, undivided attention.

According to psychologist Mihály Csíkszentmihályi, what you are experiencing in that moment is known as flow: a state of complete immersion in an activity. He describes the mental state of flow as 'being completely involved in an activity for its own sake. The ego falls away. Time flies. Every action, movement, and thought follows inevitably from the previous one, like playing jazz. Your whole being is involved, and you're using your skills to the utmost.' Flow experiences can occur in different ways for different people. Some might experience flow whilst engaging in a physical activity such as sports, dancing or running. Others might have such an experience whilst engaged in an activity such as painting, creating something, fixing something, drawing, gardening, playing an instrument or writing.

How Does it Feel to Experience Flow?
According to Csíkszentmihályi, there are ten factors that accompany the experience of flow. While many of these components may be present, it is not necessary to experience *all* of them for flow to occur:

1. clear goals that, whilst being challenging, are still attainable;
2. strong concentration and focused attention;
3. the activity is intrinsically rewarding;
4. feelings of serenity: a loss of feeling self-conscious;
5. timelessness: a distorted sense of time, feeling so focused on the present that you lose track of time passing;
6. immediate feedback;

7. knowing that the task is doable: a balance between skill level and the challenge presented;
8. feelings of personal control over the situation and the outcome;
9. lack of awareness of physical needs;
10. complete focus on the activity itself.

Finding Flow

In his book *Finding Flow*, Csíkszentmihályi explains that flow is likely to occur when an individual is faced with a task that has clear goals requiring specific responses. A game of chess is a good example of when this state might occur. For the duration of a game, the player has very specific goals and responses, allowing attention to be focused entirely on the game during the period of play.

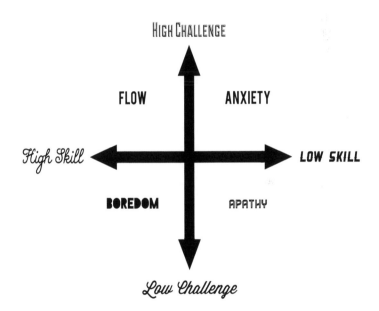

'Flow also happens when a person's skills are fully involved in overcoming a challenge that is just about manageable, so it acts as a magnet for learning new skills and increasing challenges,' Csíkszentmihályi explains. *'If challenges are too low, one gets back to flow by increasing them. If challenges are too great, one can return to the flow state by learning new skills.'*

> *Don't just read the easy stuff. You may be entertained by it,*
> *but you will never grow from it.*
> Jim Rohn

It is easy for us to see how this applies in formal and informal learning, and in interests or activities, such as sports, the arts or computer games. It's therefore important for us to take note of when we are in flow, totally absorbed in what we're doing, and find ways to replicate those experiences.

> *A pupil from whom nothing is ever demanded which*
> *he cannot do; never does all he can.*
> John Stuart Mill

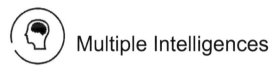 Multiple Intelligences

> *Knowing yourself is the beginning of all wisdom.*
> Aristocle

Most of us are brought up with the notion that someone who is clever or intelligent is good at reading, writing, mathematics and science. Our education system values these above other competencies. However, Howard Gardner's work has helped us to reflect on, and value, different intelligences.

What are Multiple Intelligences?

Howard Gardner's research indicates that our intelligence, or ability to understand the world around us, is complex. Some people are better at understanding some things than others. For some of us, it is relatively easy to understand how a flower grows, but it is immensely difficult for us to understand and use a musical instrument. For others, music might be easy but playing ball sports difficult.

Gardner's work identifies that, rather than having one sort of intelligence, we have several different intelligences. All of us have all these intelligences combined in different and unique ways according to the individual. We may be very strong in one area and much weaker in another. Successful people accept their strengths; they have confidence in them and play to them. They address areas they need to improve as necessary, or work with people who complement their strengths and skills (just as a team in sports is made up of people with complementary skills.). There are some intelligences that I suggest we all need to work on, such as knowing ourselves (intrapersonal intelligence), and getting on well with other people (interpersonal intelligence). More on this in Chapter fourteen; Getting On Well With People.

Here is a brief summary from which you can consider the combinations of intelligence that are found uniquely in individuals and reflect on your own strengths.

Bodily-Kinaesthetic Intelligence
Bodily intelligence means we have control over our bodies and our bodies do what we want them to do. This can include things such as hand-eye co-ordination. Individuals who are bodily intelligent are good at things that require precise movement, such as dance and sports.

Linguistic Intelligence
Linguistic intelligence is being good with words. People who are linguistically intelligent are good at reading, writing and talking about things.

Logical – Mathematical Intelligence
This includes being logical: being good with numbers and scientifically able. People who are logical are good at mathematics and other number activities such as the sciences. They also tend to be good at solving problems with logic.

Intrapersonal Intelligence
Intrapersonal intelligence means knowing ourselves: knowledge of our feelings and range of emotions. It is the capacity to discriminate between our emotions and use them as a means of understanding and guiding our behaviour. Individuals who have intrapersonal intelligence are reflective: know themselves, their strengths and

weaknesses. Their view of themselves is also very consistent with the view others have of them.

Interpersonal Intelligence
Interpersonal intelligence means being good with people. Individuals who are interpersonally intelligent are good at mixing with other people and get on well in social networks. They tend to like team games and are good at sharing. I like to think of this as 'tuning-in' with the people around us. Essential if you are going to be good at roles that involve working with people and require higher-order interpersonal intelligence.

Musical Intelligence
Being musically able means that we enjoy music and can recognise sounds, and timbre, or the quality of a tone. We can develop our technical ability and express ourselves with music.

Spatial Intelligence
Spatial intelligence is being good at spatial problem solving. People who have spatial intelligence are good at art, building things, engineering and other activities where you need to create or interpret pictures, diagrams and graphs.

Naturalist Intelligence
Naturalist intelligence is a higher-order understanding of the world around us. An individual with a high degree of naturalist intelligence is keenly aware of how to distinguish from one another the diverse plants, animals, mountains in their ecological environment.

In Howard Gardner's article, *In a Nutshell – Multiple Intelligences*, he concludes:

In brief, Multiple Intelligence theory leads to three conclusions:
1. All of us have the full range of intelligences; that is what makes us human beings, cognitively speaking.

2. No two individuals, not even identical twins, have exactly the same intellectual profile. That is because, even when the genetic material is identical, individuals have different

experiences; and those who are identical twins are often highly motivated to distinguish themselves from one another.

3. Having a strong intelligence does not mean that one necessarily acts intelligently. (What an individual may choose to do with mathematical intelligence can vary tremendously, from neuroscience to spread betting!)

Building Self-Regard with Learning

An important aspect of learning something new and gaining a skill or capability is how it boosts our self-regard. This is explored in Chapter eleven; The Power of Self-Belief, but the link between self-regard and learning is worth re-iterating. Being able to do something we couldn't previously do, from reading a book to riding a bike, from learning how to use a computer to making a meal, gives us a tremendous boost, especially if our achievement is reinforced by celebration. Individuals with low self-regard have often experienced mistakes and failure as something to be criticised, laughed at, or even punished, can gradually learn to fear failure and develop deflection techniques to avoid doing things they may not be very good at. This seriously damages their attitude to learning and capacity to learn. Some of the ways this manifests itself are by not trying, not having a go. Self-deprecation is another manifestation of this, saying things like, 'I can't do that', 'I'm rubbish at that'. It is therefore vital that we boost our self-esteem in learning new skills whenever we can, acknowledging small improvements and achievements.

Expanding Our Comfort Zone

*The man who goes farthest is generally
the one who is willing to do and dare.
The sure-thing boat never gets far from shore.*
Dale Carnegie

We all like being comfortable. Unfortunately, we can get too comfortable – in our daily routines, in our immediate community, in our relationships, in the places we regularly frequent; this limits us. In order to grow it is crucial that we break out of the mental, physical and environmental ruts that we have settled into. It takes confidence and courage to try new things, but the moment we expand our horizons, we gain confidence in all other areas of our life.

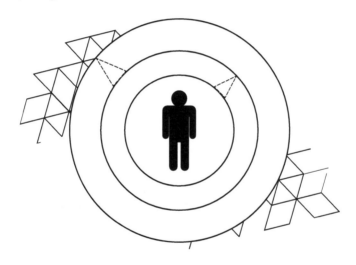

This comfort zones diagram illustrates how this works: you are at the centre, within your immediate comfort zone. This comfort zone is quite small and will start to limit your achievements over a period of time. However, it is also safe; you know exactly how everything in your life operates. Accepting challenges that help you to achieve something new will allow you to break out of your comfort bubble and develop a wider confidence zone that will enable you to cope with even more challenges, and your life will be enriched. Every time we do something new or different that challenges us, we stretch our comfort zone a little more. If you do one thing that is new it expands the whole of your comfort/confidence zone. I firmly believe that the moment we stop expanding our comfort zone it shrinks. It is a constant cycle of pushing our boundaries until we feel confident in most of our life.

Once you learn to quit, it becomes a habit.
Vincent Lombardi

Those who achieve expand their learning in areas they are passionate about to support them in reaching their vision and goals, or just to give themselves a new challenge to enable them to think more creatively and handle challenges better. They tend to have a 'helicopter view', and join the dots between things where others just don't see the connections. ('Helicopter view' is a metaphor that relates to how the helicopter rises and is able to see the bigger picture, an overview of things). They use all sorts of learning and apply it to what they want to achieve. Achieving something new brings new insights and ideas to the things you do, and helps on the journey to future goals.

To achieve beyond the norm, we need to soak up new things, try things, but not like a butterfly – flitting from one thing to the next – explore things that really interest us with passion and commitment. Think of Richard Branson and his round the world balloon challenge, and Humphrey Walters, crewing a round-the-world yacht race with no previous experience of sailing because he felt he needed a new challenge.

Successful people are always growing, developing, or sometimes reinventing themselves. They continuously improve their knowledge and skills in what they are passionate about, whether that be business, charities, sports, science, music, engineering, the arts or a particular cause. They embrace change and challenge rather than fearing it.

Be willing to be uncomfortable.
Be comfortable being uncomfortable.
It may get tough, but it's a small price to pay for
living a dream'.
Peter McWilliams

Communities of Excellence

It is no coincidence that we tend to find groups of high achievers together, geographically. If there are a number of people with technical ability, passion and a network of experienced coaches, mentors and the latest learning around them, they learn together and feed from each other. Whether it's Silicon Valley, in computing, or the British equivalent in Cambridge, groups of athletes, sports teams, academic research, medical excellence or engineering innovation, groups of focused, driven people help each other to achieve more through sharing ideas, finding ways to improve, motivating each other, challenging each other and competing. Find your communities of excellence in fields you want to pursue and those all-important people and networks who can help you excel.

Only the curious will learn and
only the resolute overcome the obstacles to learning.
The quest quotient has always excited me
more than the intelligence quotient.
Eugene S. Wilson

Affirmations
- *I am passionate about learning what I need to in order to achieve my goals.*
- *I am enthusiastically learning new things from every experience.*
- *I am exhilarated to be expanding my comfort zone with new experiences.*
- *I am loving learning from everyone around me.*
- *I am always improving how I learn.*

Nothing is difficult that is wholly desired. Trials are but lessons that you failed to learn presented once again, so where you made a faulty choice before you now can make a better one.
Unknown

 ACTION

The information shared in this chapter can help us learn and communicate more effectively. The activities below are designed to help you further develop your awareness and understanding.

1. How do you learn best?
Download a Learning Styles Questionnaire from the equipped2succeed website to help you reflect on your learning styles.

2. Reflect on your learning and write down:
Three things you've learned in the last week *and* how you will use what you learned.
Regularly ask yourself:
- 'What have I learned today?'
- 'What have I learned from that?' (successes, mistakes, experiences.)
- 'How will I use what I've learned?'

3. What are you doing to expand your comfort zone?
Think of something you would like to be able to do but haven't because you are frightened or anxious about it (or have made time, or other, excuses!).
Plan, mentally rehearse, enlist support and just do it.

There is nothing more powerful than doing it for yourself
– and knowing you can!

> ***The things that have been most valuable to me***
> ***I did not learn in school.***
> Will Smith

> *Insanity: doing the same thing over and over again*
> *and expecting different results.*
> Albert Einstein

Chapter Eleven

The Power of Self-Belief

Building high self-regard, confidence and self-belief

We are what we believe we are.
Benjamin Cardozo

self: *the distinct individuality or identity of a person; an individual's consciousness of his/her own identity or being.*

belief: *the feeling of being certain that something exists or is true; something that you believe; trust or confidence, as in a person's abilities.*

self-belief: *trust in your own abilities.*

One person with a belief, is equal to ninety-nine who have no interests.
John Stewart Mill

Successful people build and maintain belief in themselves, their goals and their abilities.

Developing and maintaining self-belief is crucial if we are to achieve our goals. Our self-belief is something we have more individual control over as we grow. There is always a debate about how much self-belief is a matter of nature or nurture but at some point we need to take responsibility for our self-belief. There is no doubt that some people seem to develop and maintain self-belief much more easily than others: as we can recognise from the differences between siblings in the same family, with very similar childhood experiences. There are those who have experienced a very negative childhood who have managed to emerge with tremendous self-belief, and also the opposite is true; there are those who appear to have had a very secure, caring childhood who are riddled with self-doubt. It is also the case that many people who have succeeded in their chosen endeavours will openly say that they have times of self-doubt. The important factor is that they don't allow their moments of self-doubt to paralyse them and prevent them from moving forward. Their self-doubt sometimes comes from humility: a desire to always do better and not settle for mediocrity. Anne Hathaway, in her acceptance speech for the Golden Globe Award she won for her role in *Les Miserables*, said:

Thank you for this blunt object which I will forever use as a weapon against self-doubt.

Our self-belief comes from the way we think about ourselves and is affected, positively or negatively, by the people around us. Unless we are one of those exceptional individuals whose self-belief can withstand being surrounded by negativity and doubters and come out saying, 'I'll show you'. Our self-belief is supported by our 'self-talk' and is linked to the positive, can-do attitude described in Chapter seven; *Being Positive*. To develop self-belief, we need to accentuate what we can do rather than what we can't, and keep in mind our limitless potential.

'I will become what I deserve' is a line from Ben Howard's *The Fear*. In other words, I will become what I think about, what I feel, because that's what I'll attract to me. And it's vital that we believe we deserve our vision and believe in our capacity to realise that positive future for ourselves. In this chapter, we explore maintaining high self-regard and the belief that we deserve, and can achieve, the things we want to be, do, have.

It's crucial, if we are to realise our goals and be, do, have what we really want, to believe in ourselves, and our infinite capacity. A big goal is a light toward which we are heading, and above all else we need to believe we can reach it, taking one step at a time, and believing in our capacity to succeed at each next step along the road, even when things get challenging.

If we find we don't have belief in what we're striving for, we need to change our goals or change our thinking. If we are to develop and maintain positive, affirming relationships, personally, socially, in learning and work contexts, we need to have high self-regard and self-belief, or we are in danger of letting people limit, humiliate or bully us and we may not make the most of opportunities.

Self-belief and confidence are often used to mean the same thing. However, the distinct difference for me is that one is internal and one is external. Self-belief is internal: what we really believe about ourselves, and our capacity to realise our goals. Confidence is the belief in our abilities that we choose to show to the world. There are people who appear to have great confidence, but who, when we scratch the surface, are actually riddled with self-doubt. Arrogance comes into this mix here and I am always having debates with people about where the line is between confidence and arrogance.

Like confidence, arrogance is what we choose to show to the world. Confidence and arrogance are on the same spectrum; the line between them is sometimes fine, and can easily be crossed. Arrogance may mask self-doubt, rather than indicate self-belief.

confidence
trust and self-belief
in one's own ability

arrogance
an exaggerated
opinion of one's own V
importance or ability

People who believe in themselves and are confident appear comfortable in their own skin and are often humble rather than arrogant. As Paul McKenna says in his book, *Instant Confidence: The Power to Go for Anything You Want*, **Have you ever heard someone say about a person 'they seem comfortable in their own skin'? This is the essence of natural confidence – feeling a level of comfort with yourself that can withstand the slings and arrows of outrageous fortune and carry you forward to the life of your dreams.**

People who are arrogant see themselves as better than those around them and can show this in their language and body language. They focus solely on themselves and their performance, not recognising others' contributions and value, sometimes putting others down and abdicating responsibility when things go wrong.

> **Confidence comes not from always being right, but from not fearing to be wrong.**
> Peter McIntyre

 # Self-image - Self-regard - Self-belief

Our self-belief is within and is intrinsically linked to our self-image and self-regard. Definitions of self-image and self-regard vary, but I define them as:

- self-image is your view of yourself;
- self-regard (or self-esteem) is the evaluation of that view.

A positive self-image and high self-regard supports building and maintaining our self-belief.

People with high self-regard, who believe in themselves:

- tell themselves they can: their self-talk is positive;
- are assertive, not passive or aggressive; they calmly and strongly state their views and do what is best for themselves and those around them. As Henry C. Link says:

> **While one person hesitates because he feels inferior, the other is busy making mistakes and becoming superior.**

We all find that life events, such as failing an exam, failing an interview, losing a friend, performing poorly in something we love, losing a job, ending a relationship or being bereaved, can give our confidence a huge knock. However, high self-regard can act as a buffer to absorb these knocks and help us bounce back.

Signs of High Self-Regard

When asked to do something:	Confidently say you can do it, or say you'll have a go, or say you don't want to do it and give reasons.
How you feel about yourself:	Feel you have value and make a contribution. Feel you can achieve and are learning all the time to do things better.
When you need help:	Are prepared to ask for help and support from people who have the right knowledge, skills and experience to help; without being needy or dependent.
When things go wrong:	Acknowledge when things go wrong and accept responsibility. Learn from mistakes and don't keep making the same mistake.
When you have a difficulty with someone or someone tries to put you down:	Respond assertively with people, being calm and clear with your language, remaining confident in your own value and treating people with polite respect.

Remember, there are no mistakes, only lessons.
Love yourself, trust your choices, and everything is possible.
Cherie Carter-Scott

People with high self-regard also tend to be assertive:

Assertive – being 'for real' and strong	Body language	Actions
Keen to stand up for your rights while accepting that others have rights, too.	Enough eye contact to let people know you are serious.	Lots of listening; seek to understand.
	Moderate, neutral tone of voice.	Treat people with respect.
	Moderate, open body posture.	Prepared to compromise; solution-focused.
	Body language in tune with spoken words.	Prepared to state and explain you want.
		Straight and to the point without being abrupt. Prepared to persist for what you want.

Signs of Low Self-Regard – Two Poles

Quiet (timid)	Loud (brash)
Say can't do things (believe everyone else can).	Say can do things (but not prepared to be tested).
Feel worthless, useless and tell you that.	Have to tell everyone how marvellous they are.
Are constantly needy.	Don't want help – think to accept help is a sign of weakness; people will realise they are worthless.
Don't admit things are wrong.	Constantly reinforce things are wrong. Blame others.
Are frightened to say anything to people who put them down.	Put people 'in their place'. Reinforce their own worth by (often inappropriately) telling people they are in charge.

Low self-regard is evident in a variety of ways, sometimes apparently opposite behaviours showing the same feelings of low self-worth, with timid behaviour at one end of the spectrum and arrogant, brash behaviour at the other. We find these behaviours (and everything in between) in children, young people and adults alike. Low self-regard is a feeling of inferiority or inadequacy. Behaviour can include being 'needy' or using avoidance tactics to not let others see your inadequacies. It takes a self-confident person to say 'I haven't got a clue, explain it to me' without feeling inadequate in some way.

The impact of praise and criticism on our self-regard

The praise and criticism of those around us, those with whom we have the strongest emotional bond, those who have some authority over us and those we admire, has the potential to have tremendous impact on our self-regard and self-belief, especially when we are young. One study maintained that, praise needs to outweigh criticism 15:1 if we are not going to damage an individual's self-regard. However accurate that is, it gives us food for thought. There is no doubt that both can have tremendous impact on individuals, and an even greater impact when we add in the uniquely close emotional relationship between close family members parents, children and siblings and partners. It also has a disproportionate impact between those in positional power and those over which they have power.

It's useful to consider what effective praise and criticism looks like so we can praise and criticise appropriately and filter and question ineffective praise and criticism from others. Praise needs to have purpose, be constructive and useful. A pre-occupied 'Well done', when it's obvious we're not paying attention, doesn't do it. Empty praise is almost as bad as thoughtless criticism. It is the same with criticism; it needs to be constructive, useful, and framed in the positive to enable the recipient to develop their understanding of continuous improvement, of being reflective and using constructive criticism as part of that reflection.

Praise needs to:

be sincere: not just an empty gesture – individuals spot this a mile away and it has no positive impact.

be specific: praising a specific action or achievement.

encourage: particular performance or behaviour.

promote autonomy: encourage individuals to take responsibility and be independent.

enhance competence: recognise specific competence and give a pointer for improvement.

convey attainable standards and expectations: recognise achievement and reinforce expectations

celebrate success: success deserves recognition and celebration.

I believe in always balancing encouragement, challenge and support to enable improvement. Recognising improvement and celebrating success balances the challenge.

Criticism needs to:

be for an individual's benefit: whether that's for them

personally, or within the context of their relationships or role.

framed in the positive: what we want to see, rather than what we don't want to see. What is the point of criticising unless it's to improve something? We therefore need to recognise positives, effort and prior achievement before suggesting improvements.

come with a solution: if you haven't got a solution, don't say anything at all, unless it's to ask questions to help people come to their own solutions.

be specific: focus on a specific area for improvement, not a long list of moans.

come with a question: too many times, criticism comes with 'telling', 'What you should do is ...' Improvement is much more likely to come by starting with a coaching approach, 'What do you think you could do to improve ...?'.

offer help: if criticism is followed by, 'What can I do to help you with this?', it reinforces that we're serious and shows we care and are willing to help.

encourage: a particular attitude, way of thinking, skill, performance or behaviour.

promote autonomy: encourage individuals to take responsibility and be independent.

enhance competence: recognise specific competence/s that individuals need to develop, for their own benefit and the benefit of those around them. This includes developing emotional and social competence, work ethic, and so on.

convey attainable standards and expectations: recognise achievement and reinforce expectations.

> *Sandwich every bit of criticism between two*
> *thick layers of praise.*
> Mary Kay Ash

All in all, praise and criticism needs to be balanced. Remember: praise tends to bring praise and criticism tends to bring criticism and it's getting both in balance that leads to growth. We need to recognise valuable criticism and learn from it. We need to challenge inappropriate criticism with calm, focused questioning or keep our protective 'bubble' firmly in place!

Ditch the Doubters

One of the things we need to guard against is having people around us who 'put us down'. None of us need people around us who negatively put us down and limit our ambition from the standpoint of their negativity or fear. This limiting of ambition is often framed or phrased as protecting us: making us 'be realistic'. Others sometimes do this due to their own low self-esteem. They need to 'keep you in your place' or 'put you in your place' because of their own insecurities.

If you have friends in your circle like this, move away. If those close to you have people in their lives like this, help them to guard against their negative impact. It is more challenging to limit the impact of family members like this. However, we can mentally move away and limit their negative impact on us, using our protective bubble.

 Building Our Self-Belief

My professional and personal experience has given me some indicators of how we can build and maintain our self-belief. Mine has certainly ebbed and flowed over the years in different circumstances. In addition to what is outlined in the above, here are a few things that I believe are important to keep in mind to build and maintain the self-belief that is essential for us to realise our potential:

- Recognise we are individual and cannot measure ourselves against others' experience and skills. We all have different skills and experiences. Just take opportunities to grow.

- Be willing to try new things, and expand your comfort zone.

- Develop your emotional intelligence and assertiveness to tune-in with the situations you face, and amend your behaviour and approach accordingly, especially using challenge and support to help development.

- Speak to others as equals, without unnecessary deference, no matter what their position.

- **Expect that you can and will**, in whatever context, and it's amazing what you can do if you expect it of yourself. There is nothing like achievement in anything to build self-belief

- Don't allow yourself to be limited by others expectations.

- The other side of the expectation coin is don't burden yourself with disappointment. When we fail at something or can't understand something, we tend to feel inadequate in some way. If we allow that feeling to be compounded by others it can do untold damage to our self-regard and self-belief.

- Accept that some things are going to be challenging. Rather than being paralysed by fear, find ways to get round, through or over challenges. Learn from others and ask for help.

- Failing is an essential learning experience and helps build resilience. Set failure in context; don't view it as something final, but rather as part of the way we grow.

> *Our greatest glory is not in never failing,*
> *but in rising up every time we fail.*
> Ralph Waldo Emerson

Michael Jordan is one of the all-time greats of basketball, and yet he was dropped from his school basketball team and told he wasn't good enough. It's a good job Michael Jordan didn't accept the expectations of others!

> *If you accept the expectations of others, especially negative*
> *ones, then you will never change the outcome.*
> Michael Jordan

Courage

To pursue what we really want to do, and achieve anything of worth, we need to be courageous: willing to try and unafraid to fail. When we're young, this can mean being courageous in learning. At any age it can be embracing new experiences, challenging someone who is intimidating us, taking a job in another city or country.

To live a creative life, we must lose our fear of being wrong.
Joseph Chilton Pearce

Affirmations
- *I am comfortably handling challenges.*
- *I am appreciating my skills.*
- *I am loving how confident I feel.*
- *I am developing my self-belief every day.*
- *I am confidently achieving my goals.*
- *I am valuing my achievements.*
- *I am building self-belief in myself and the people around me.*
- *I am proudly making a valuable contribution.*
- *I am confidently building my skills and learning every day.*

 ACTION

1. Reinforce your positive image. Write down three of your:
- best physical attributes;
- best mental abilities;
- best financial moves;
- most unusual characteristics;
- best general human attributes;
- best social skills;
- most important interests;
- your most important values

Keep your list where you can see it frequently – in hard copy and electronically.

2. Praise V Criticism Diary

Keep a diary for a few weeks in either a notebook or on the electronic device you use most; anything that's going to be handy. The purpose of this is to help you reflect on the way you receive praise and criticism, how you use it, how it affects you and how helpful it is for you. Also reflect on the way you give praise and criticism yourself. Is it helpful for the individuals on the receiving end of your comments? What we think we do and what we actually do may well be different.

3. Being Comfortable Being Uncomfortable

1. Think of circumstances when you feel most comfortable in your daily life: most content and confident.
    Think of the feelings you associate with these times.

2. Think of circumstances when you feel least comfortable in your daily life: ill-at-ease, anxious, worried or frightened.
    Reflect on what you can do to overcome this.

Change the circumstances or change the way you respond to the circumstances.

4. Act As If

When we're feeling inadequate and lacking confidence, we can 'act as if'. Act as if we are good at something; act as if we're confident doing something. This makes us reflect on the thinking, language, body language and behaviour associated with what we're working on and helps us build the belief in ourselves. If we take on the thinking, language and the body language of someone who can do something, we start to find we're more comfortable and confident doing it ourselves. This is just another version of role-play or taking on the behaviours of role models.

Life is not easy for any of us.
But what of that?
We must have perseverance and above all
confidence in ourselves.
We must believe that we are gifted for something and that
this thing must be attained.
Marie Curie

Marie Curie was a Polish physicist and chemist, working mainly in France, who is famous for her pioneering research on radioactivity. She was the first woman to win a Nobel Prize, the only woman to win in two fields, and the only person to win in multiple sciences. Her name lives on with the Marie Curie Cancer Care Charity.

Chapter Twelve

Manage Stress (better)

Managing ourselves effectively for wellbeing

manage: *to bring about or succeed in accomplishing, sometimes despite difficulty or hardship;*
to take charge or care of.

stress: *a specific response by the body to a stimulus, such as fear or pain, that disturbs or interferes with the normal physiological equilibrium of an organism;*
physical, mental, or emotional strain or tension;
great worry caused by a difficult situation, or something that causes this condition.

better: *of a higher standard, or more suitable or more effective than other things;*
of superior quality or excellence.

Successful people minimise the negative effects of stress; they do it naturally and instinctively or they develop strategies to manage it effectively. Their positive mental attitude and their focus on the future help them to avoid being overwhelmed or paralysed by the anxiety of challenges. They get things in perspective and see beyond the immediate challenge. In this chapter, we consider the impact of general stress in our lives and how we can effectively equip ourselves to minimise the negative effects of stress and perform at our best, especially when it matters most.

In workshops, people sometimes want to be clear about the difference is between anxiety and stress. In summary: the symptoms of anxiety and stress are driven by the same chemical reaction; stress is a normal response to a threatening situation, (or a situation we perceive as threatening), and anxiety is largely caused by (excessive) worry.

 ## So, what do we mean by stress?

One of the most commonly accepted definitions of stress (mainly attributed to Richard S Lazarus) is that *stress is a condition or feeling experienced when a person perceives that demands exceed the personal and social resources the individual is able to mobilise.*

A growing awareness has meant that stress has become much more widely recognised and talked about. All of us experience it to different degrees, whether we are parents, shop assistants, sports men and women, computer analysts, teachers, nurses or company directors. Stress affects us all at different times and in different ways, whether we recognise it or not.

In fields of endeavour that involve public performance, such as sports and the arts, stress can manifest itself as performance anxiety, and this is akin to the sort of stress we feel when going into an examination, an interview or making an important presentation. In Chapter six; *Use Your Amazing Winning Brain*, we explored how to perform at our best under pressure and when it matters most. A major contributory factor to peak performance is effectively managing stress and performance anxiety.

Imbalance is usually a feature of stress. A feeling that things are out of control and we can't cope is a major cause of the angst and feelings of paralysis associated with stress. We may have too much to do and too little time: too much freedom and too little direction, too much responsibility and too little power. Change can often create a strong sense of imbalance: we were in control, then things change, and we feel out of control, and our security may seem threatened. The more we know about ourselves, the quicker we are able to define fresh frameworks that make us feel secure again. If a key indicator of stress is feeling overwhelmed and out of control, there is little wonder in the rise of its recognition in recent times. The pace at which we live has changed, with more and more of us juggling infinite numbers of roles and responsibilities. We are bombarded by information, a plethora of communication tools, and we are continually trying to find a balance between too little and too much information, and too little and too much communication. This is demanding.

Almost all of us have mobile phone: some of us more than one. We are accessible 24/7 by telephone, text and email for the communication we want to be available for, as well as that which we need to carefully manage and moderate. We can also be absorbed in a plethora of social media and continuously access infinite amounts of digital information. Overload is a natural extension of this.

In 2010, Google CEO Eric Schmidt famously said:
Every two days now we create as much information as we did from the dawn of civilization up until 2003.
Let me repeat that: we create as much information in two days now as we did from the dawn of man through 2003.

To make it even more personal, in his book *Information Anxiety* (1989), Richard Wurman claimed that,
The weekday edition of The New York Times contains more information than the average person in 17th-century England was likely to come across in a lifetime.

Stress was not used as an expression to describe that state of heightened intolerance, feeling overwhelmed or general grumpiness until relatively recently. Some people still refuse to accept the term stress as an expression that relates to them. Some people recognise it but see it as part of life and don't seek to address it.

Situations and circumstances affect each of us differently, and it's vital that we recognise and address it when things affect us negatively. How we respond as individuals to life's challenges varies. What some will regard as horribly stressful, others will find exhilarating. So perception affects our response and stress levels in different situations.

We therefore need to recognise what affects us negatively, how it affects us and develop the tools to handle situations better so that we are not limited by negative stress. This doesn't mean avoiding things that 'stress' us. Sometimes, a continuous avoidance of stressful situations just brings up more issues later, or puts a limit on us achieving our potential. Continuously avoiding things we don't like or find stressful can result in us failing to expand our comfort zones. It can limit our horizons.

I have learned to recognise that I feel stress when things negatively affect me over which I have some control and choice. Feeling anger or hurt is not the same as feeling stress. I feel anger, sadness or pain over things I can't do anything about: injustice, unfairness, and when there are people and things that negatively affect my family and friends. The power of empathy means I feel their pain. When my actions and decisions could have been better, when overwhelmed by work that I could manage better, when trying to do too much, juggling work and family and feeling I'm not doing either to the best of my ability, when people I trusted let me down, when trying to keep a business going for the benefit of all involved, swimming hard against a negative economic climate, then I have felt the negative effects of stress. I have needed to develop and use all the tools described in this chapter at different times and, sometimes, all at once.

Of course, there are positive effects from 'stress'; it gives us our motivation, our 'get-up-and-go' or drive to make things happen. Being too 'laid back' can result in not putting in the effort to achieve our goals. A stimulating amount of challenge can make us: work more efficiently; get new ideas; take more risks; have more energy; feel fine on less sleep; feel worthy; feel fit and assertive; have more confidence and more enthusiasm. In short, having lots of stimulation and relishing opportunities can make us thrive and, in general, enjoy life more.

However, when stress becomes too much, we can: become snappy and irritable; make poor decisions; experience mood swings; have trouble sleeping, or sleep more than usual; avoid seeing friends and doing things. We can: smoke more; drink more alcohol and coffee; eat to excess, or not eat enough; have a whole range of physical symptoms such as headache, back-ache and neck-ache, lapses of memory and loss of concentration, stomach upsets and panic attacks. Signs in our behaviour that we may be under stress include: lots of blinking; fidgeting; talking incessantly; frowning unconsciously; repeated swallowing, sighing or licking our lips; making obsessive notes and lists, in our heads or on paper.

I write this as someone who has done all of the above: not recognised stress; suffered from most of the negative symptoms at some time or other; allowed herself to be overwhelmed by it, and allowed it to negatively affect relationships. I had let stress reach unacceptable and unhealthy levels on occasions, prior to my 'melt down'. It's when I became very sick that I decided to find out more about stress and how to manage it more effectively.

Are you aware of when you are negatively affected by stress?

Are your own strategies to manage stress well developed?

Are you spotting stress in those around you and helping effectively manage it?

What follows in this chapter is some general information and strategies that have helped me, and others, to recognise and effectively manage stress and performance anxiety.

Let's break down what stress is. In my experience, it is always easier to prevent something or address something if we can break it down and reflect on exactly how it relates to us, and those close to us.

Major Sources of Stress

Survival Stress

This is when we are in a physically or emotionally threatening situation, and our body adapts to help us react more effectively to meet the threat. However, our brain cannot distinguish between this and other stresses so it can put our body into unhealthy survival mode that is designed to get us through a certain incident, over prolonged periods of time.

Internally-generated Stress

This can come from worrying about events beyond our control, from a tense, hurried approach to life, or from relationship problems caused by our own behaviour.

Environmental stress

This can come from:

- crowding and invasion of personal space;
- insufficient working and living space;
- noise and pollution;
- dirty / untidy conditions.

Chemical and nutritional stress

The food you eat may contribute to stress. Examples of stressors are caffeine, sugar and salt. Smoking also puts your body under chemical stress.

Lifestyle and job stress

Examples of these are financial or relationship problems, ill-health, time pressures and deadlines, redundancy, looking for a job.

Fatigue and overwork

This manifests itself as a constant feeling of tiredness, due to working too many hours, or trying to fit too many things into the hours.

Stress Indicators

Physical – Behavioural – Emotional

I include this list as a reminder that it is important to recognise the early signs of stress in ourselves, and in those around us. In order to manage stress effectively it is most important that we spot the warning signs.

Physical

Tight chest, rapid swallowing, palpitations, indigestion, stomach cramp, shoulder/neck or back pain, persistent headaches, chronic sinus problems, humming in the ears, frequent viral infections, weight loss/gain, skin problems, tired eyes/visual disturbances, body stiffness, attacks of dizziness, frequent pins and needles.

Behavioural:

Poor concentration, inability to listen well, forgetfulness, over activity, restlessness, talking too much, nervous habits such as nail biting, inability to make decisions or sort priorities, poor planning, reluctance to delegate, over sensitivity to events and situations, increase in phobic fears, anxieties and obsessions, increase in alcohol, sugar, nicotine intake, insomnia, nightmares, loss of libido, unkempt appearance, loss of control over money, over cautious, over protective.

Emotional:

Increase in anxiety, fearfulness, easily hurt or upset, tearful, feeling irritable, lacking in confidence, a sense of worthlessness and apathy, confused, overwhelmed, humourless, getting over excited, generally melancholic or depressed, mood swings, feeling embarrassed or ashamed, feeling controlled by others, gloomy about the future, cynical attitudes, obsessive thoughts, more angry and emotionally reactive.

If you recognise any of these, start doing something about it **now**: there's lots you can do!

The good news is that we can all take control of our responses to stress.

Feeling overwhelmed is like the little dancing
top on the pressure cooker.
It is a safety device that is warning us to take notice.
We can ignore the warning and if we do, something will blow.
Anne Wilson Schaef

 # Managing Stress Better

Here are some simple ways to improve our ability to manage the stresses of life.

Remember that every time you think a situation is stressful,
your brain tries to help – so it starts the stress responses.
Give your brain the right information and manage your brain,
rather than letting your brain manage you!

Choosing to

One of the things that has helped me to manage my stress levels more effectively is changing my mindset to 'I choose to...' rather than 'I have to...' or 'I need to...'. We choose to do almost everything we do. We quite often say, 'I have to do this' or 'I have to do that' when really we don't 'have to' at all: **we can choose.**

There are choices and consequences, and we make choices about what we do based on the consequences. I found my stress levels massively reducing as soon as I started thinking that I make a choice about everything I do and consciously saying to myself 'I choose to' rather than 'I have to'. It works with chores as well as work.

Choices and Consequences

If we don't want to study for an examination, what are the consequences?

With some exams, the consequences of a low grade may be

minimal. With other exams, it may mean not being able to progress to the next level and study something we really want to, or not being able to follow our chosen profession.

If we don't like our job, we have some choices
We just need to work through the consequences of all these choices on us, and those around us:

- just stick at it, getting more stressed about doing something that makes us unhappy;
- don't turn up for work;
- do it badly so we get sacked;
- resign without a job to go to;
- set a goal and action plan to change jobs to do something we want to do; use relaxation, visualisation and mental rehearsal to help us see ourselves achieving our goal and do what it takes to make the change!

We all need to take control and feel in control of everything we do, and say 'I choose to … do this job, go to work early, help my family, take my parents out, exercise'.

You'll be amazed how liberating it is to adopt the 'I choose to' mindset and how much better you will feel.

Attitude is more important than the past, than education, than money, than circumstances, than what other people think or say or do. It is more important than appearance, giftedness, or skill. It will make or break a company, a church, a home.
Charles Swindoll

Learn to Relax
It is essential that we recognise that relaxation is within our own power and not something that is dependent on external circumstances.

Sometimes, we have very little control over external circumstances, but we always have the power to decide what's going on in our mind. If we systematically learn to use that power positively, we can teach ourselves to be calm and relax at any given moment. When we are calm and daydreaming, the brain goes into a state that makes the body release more serotonin and, thereby, aids relaxation. I have effectively practiced this to lower my stress levels since I learned about it. However, this systematic relaxation is not just important for our general relaxation and wellbeing, it is also essential to maximise our power to perform at our best under pressure when it matters most. When under pressure to perform at our best, we need to be focused but calm, as described in Chapter six; *Use Your Amazing Winning Brain*.

As with any other skill or habit, we use it or lose it, so we need to learn to regularly practice R – V – MR: relaxation, visualisation and mental rehearsal.

Throughout the day, take mini-breaks (time for yourself): sit down, slowly take a deep breath in, hold it and then let it out slowly. At the same time, let your shoulders droop down, smile (this is important, as it encourages the release of endorphins, natural tranquilisers) and say something like, 'I am relaxed'. I learned a better breathing technique when someone was demonstrating for me how deliberate breathing can lower our heart rate. I was hooked up to a monitor and told to breathe in, counting internally to ten, and breath out, again internally counting to ten. If we repeat this five times, our heart rate lowers and we become more relaxed.

Of course, like with everything else, we get out what we put in! By this I mean it's important to think about what we drink to aid the power of relaxation. We can't practice effective relaxation if we're pumped full of caffeine. This was a really important factor for me learning to manage stress: limiting my caffeine intake to be able to use relaxation techniques to effectively manage my stress levels.

Alongside relaxation is good quality rest. The importance of good quality rest for our health and wellbeing is described in Chapter thirteen; *Maximise Energy*.

Practice Acceptance

To minimise our stress levels it is important to accept the things we cannot change.

Many of us get distressed over things that we can't change, like some else's actions, feelings or beliefs. We can, of course to a certain extent, affect others actions and behaviours, but my experience is that being irate and angry as an unmeasured, stressed response does no good for us and makes no difference to what we're railing against. It is only natural to feel distress when faced with things we deem cruel or unfair. Personally, I become most distressed by any cruelty or unfairness towards children, whether it's a news report of an atrocity or seeing a parent in a supermarket treating their child cruelly or unfairly. Empowering children is my passion, but I am not going to change the behaviour of one parent or one group of people by getting worked up and ranting. I may feel momentarily better, but have I done any good? What I can do is use all my experience to play a small part in positively affecting the way we treat children and young people, and contributing to the body of knowledge on how best to nurture our children.

Some of the questions I ask myself are:

How important is it?
Can I change anything?
Who can help me with this?

In summary, it's vital that we recognise and accept the things we can't change, things that are truly beyond our control, and focus our energies on positively affecting the things we can change.

Talk Rationally to Ourselves

As mentioned above, it's crucial that we get used to having those reflective conversations with ourselves to help us get things in perspective. Ask yourself what real impact the stressful situation will have on you in a day or a week, and see if you can let the negative thoughts go. Think through the situation: is it your problem or someone else's? If it is yours, approach it calmly and firmly; planning and setting specific goals and actions will help with this.

Rather than condemning yourself, thinking of past mistakes or 'should haves', think about what you have learned and make plans for the future.

Keep an eye on perfection – seeking perfection in everything limits our forward movement. Set realistic steps towards your goals – remember that everyone makes mistakes; break tasks into smaller units and do important ones first.

Get Organised

I am not the worlds best at routine, and am always overly ambitious about how much I can achieve in a day. However, I recognise that having a realistic programme of daily activities that includes time for work, relationships, family, rest, eating the right things, physical activity and relaxation is really important if we are to achieve our best and manage our stress. For one thing, achievement is a great antidote to the negative impact of stress. Getting things done, tackling challenges rather than leaving things undone, helps us to feel good and relax. There are mixed views on the value of putting everything in our diary and on to-do lists, but for me they are invaluable; once everything is on a list, it takes away the burden of remembering what needs to be done. And ticking things off is great! It is in our nature to focus on the things we like and understand and to avoid the things we find challenging. However, if we can approach those things we least like to do with the attitude of 'I choose to do this' rather than 'I have to', it really helps. We feel tremendous benefit as soon as we tackle some of those challenging things and take steps forward or completely tick them off the list.

Over the years, I have increasingly recognised the importance of my surroundings. That old adage 'a place for everything and everything in its place' has made more sense; for electronic filing, as well as knowing where I've put things at home. I am not a natural when it comes to being tidy or filing but recognise that wasted time and energy looking for things can add to my stress levels. Straightening things up helps us to use our time and energy as effectively and efficiently as possible, as long as we don't get caught by perfection and spend too much time tidying, and too little time doing those important things that contribute to achieving our goals.

Exercise

There is no doubt that physical activity is vital for us in all sorts of ways, health, vitality, thinking, and it is especially important to prevent, and provide relief from, stress. Not only does exercise remove you from the stressful situation, just walking or stretching will help the body recover its normal state. As described in more detail in Chapter thirteen; *Maximise Energy*, it's important for us to find an exercise regime that suits us, whether that's walking, jogging, sport, dancing, swimming or yoga; we find that our energy levels increase and we reduce the cycle of stress.

Getting out: walking, jogging, running, cycling, really helps our sanity and ability to think clearly about all that 'stuff' we face. 'Stuff' is a much less threatening word than 'problems' or 'issues', and relegates challenges to their rightful place: obstacles that challenge our creativity to get round, over, under or through, but don't stop us. There are always solutions to 'stuff', and we're good at coming up with solutions and making things happen. It's just that when we're in the middle of so much 'stuff', flying at us from all angles, it's hard to use the best of our creative juices or little grey cells! Getting out will help that. I know that one of the effects of stress is feeling that we want to shut ourselves away and sleep. When we're awake, we just get ourselves back on the treadmill of busy activity, feeling overwhelmed but unable to stop for fear of getting further behind. Taking a walk or some form of exercise helps us break that cycle: half an hour a day makes all the difference or taking ten minutes walking round the block when we're stuck on something at work. I only wish I'd learned this sooner in my working life!

Reduce Time Urgency

I have always given myself 'just enough' time or, on many (or most) occasions, not enough time, to fit everything in: to get to appointments or to get home to get the children to activities in the rush hour on a Friday evening. I have also consistently overestimated the amount I can achieve in an hour, a day, a week. This causes stress. We deal with it (or not) at the time, but we pay the price: unless we are so laid back that we don't care about being late for things. It's crucial that we find ourselves time to do what we've committed to do. Humphrey Walters, who sailed round the world as part of a challenge has a rule: 'Aim to be 20 minutes early at sea and 15 minutes early on land'. This takes away the stress and enables us to deal with any last-minute eventuality.

It's important that we learn to allow plenty of time to get things done: plan and aim to pace, not race.

> *Using our personal resources carefully today will make us*
> *stronger for what we need to do tomorrow.*
> *How do we marshal our personal resources?*
> *Our wit, our charm, our intelligence, our wisdom,*
> *our clarity of vision, our energy – we have them all.*
> Anne Wilson Schaef

Disarm Yourself
I find this really difficult. I am passionate about what I do, and have always felt compelled to challenge anything and everything that limits people rather than focusing on the specific areas where I am likely to have most impact. This doesn't always get results and, on occasions afterwards, I have gone over and over situations, identifying how I could have behaved differently to bring about a better outcome. This generates stress! It's a much more effective and healthier approach to assess each situation according to its demands and be very targeted and focused in our efforts. We don't have to raise our voice in every conversation, get our point across to everyone. We can leave our weapons behind when the situation is a lost cause and focus on where and how we can be of most benefit.

Chilling is Okay
It's taken me years to rid myself of the guilt of just chilling. For example, I walk at pace everywhere. Having a quiet, undemanding time is important for anyone, and we need to do this for ourselves and recognise the need in our family and friends. Balance is, yet again, important here, and we need to also ensure that we don't take chilling to an extreme that means we lose focus on our goals. Chilling is one of the antidotes to hard work, not a replacement for it.

Watch Our Habits

Habits, positive or negative, take hold, and it is crucial to develop positive habits to keep us physically and mentally healthy and fit. Eating sensibly is crucial. We all tend to use comfort food, in some form or other, when we're stressed: sweets, chocolate, excess of caffeine, fatty foods, alcohol and so on. Our destructive 'Chimp'* tells us it's okay as we've had a hard day. This invariably gives us an immediate boost in energy or mood, only to be replaced by feeling even worse. A good diet, as discussed in Chapter thirteen; *Maximise Energy*, provides the energy we need during the day. We need to minimise alcohol intake as we need to be mentally and physically alert to deal with stress. Excessive caffeine and sugar can cause excitement and can make us hyperactive; that certainly is the case with me. Cigarettes also restrict blood circulation and affect the stress response.

* 'The Chimp' as defined by Dr Steve Peters in his brilliant book, *'The Chimp Paradox – The Mind Management Programme for Confidence, Success and Happiness'*: *'The Chimp is the emotional machine that we all possess. It thinks independently from us and can make decisions. It offers emotional thoughts and feelings that can be very constructive or very destructive; it is not good or bad, it is a Chimp. The Chimp Paradox is that it can be your best friend or your worst enemy, even at the same time'*. I have used this phrase as it's one to which I think we can all relate.

Talk to Friends and Have Fun

Daily pleasant, positive conversations, regular social events, sharing deep feelings and thoughts, aid wellbeing and reduce stress really well. In his book, *The Outliers: The Story of Success*, Malcolm Gladwell writes about some research undertaken by Dr Stewart Wolf and his friend and sociologist, John Bruhn, in the 1950s, into why the population of a small town, Roseto, Pennsylvania, appeared to be so much healthier than anywhere else.

'In Roseto, virtually no one under fifty-five had died of a heart attack or showed any signs of heart disease. For men over sixty-five, the death rate from heart disease in Roseto was roughly half that of the

United States as a whole. The death rate from all causes in Roseto, in fact, was 30–35% lower than expected'.

He goes on, 'There was no suicide, no alcoholism, no drug addiction, and very little crime. They didn't have anyone on welfare. Then we looked at peptic ulcers. They didn't have any of those either. These people were dying of old age. That's it'.

The people of Roseto originated in Roseto Valafortore, in the Appennine foothills of the Italian province of Foggia. Their diet wasn't classed as healthy; many smoked heavily and their genetic make-up was similar to their relatives living in other parts of America who did not have the same health profile. They eventually discovered their health was attributed to their social structure: extended families, cooking together, looking after one another, and incredibly impressive social and community structures, 'twenty-two separate civic organizations in a town of just under two thousand people'. This meant people socialised, had fun, belonged and felt secure. '…. the Rosetans had created a powerful, protective social structure capable of insulating them from the pressures of the modern world.' The strong community spirit and social life they had created had incredible benefits on their health, in part, by protecting them from the negative effects of stress.

In my over-active, focused daily routine, it's only in recent years I have truly valued just chatting without a specific purpose and agenda, and learned to feel that it's okay to phone someone for a chat rather than for a particular purpose. It's only now that I properly understand the value of what Wolf and Bruhn found in that Rosetan town: my social network within and beyond my family, and informal chat.

Laughter is also especially good for reducing stress as this releases endorphins that make us feel better, and having fun with family and friends is crucial (as is learning to laugh at ourselves). We can make lots of things we do fun, with a bit of imagination, and the benefits are good for us all. The people of Roseta got this and it was the biggest factor in their health, wellbeing and longevity.

Good friends are good for your health.
Irwin Sarason

Affirmations

- *I am positive and feeling great;*
- *I am managing my stress better all the time.*
- *I am loving the feeling of remaining calm and positive.*
- *I am enjoying the liberating feeling of consciously choosing everything I do in my life.*
- *I am feeling amazing after socialising with friends.*
- *I am feeling tremendous, having fun with my family.*

 ACTION

1. Deliberately relax regularly. Try the free relaxation download link on the equipped2succeed website, to help you minimise the negative effects of stress.

2. Think of the times you experience feelings or reactions of negative stress. Note that our reactions to stress can often be delayed and may come out at other times; if we're feeling stressed by work, we may not lose our temper or 'snap' with our work colleagues, but with our partner or family later.

3. Look at the stress indicators above and use them to help you reflect on your stress levels. Knowing exactly what you're dealing with will help you do something about it.

4. Use the Stress Quiz: How Stressed Are You? on the equipped2succeed website to have an indication of your stress levels.
   What do you think causes your negative stressful reactions?
   What are you doing about it?

5. Look at the Managing Stress Tips and decide which ones are best for you to start implementing.

6. Use a goal-setting template on the equipped2succeed website. Write a goal and action plan to manage stress/performance anxiety better.

Only the Individual Can Eliminate the Negative
Effects of Stress in Themselves,
and we are in the Best Place to
Coach Our Children to Manage Stress Effectively

relax: take time every day to relax and do mini relaxations throughout the day – even in the toilet;

work on your positive attitude: choose to do everything you do;

look at your diet and make sure you are eating healthily;

exercise your body and your mind regularly – choose the exercise you like;

change what you do and how you do it to eliminate the negative effects of stress;

and

HAVE FUN!

Chapter Thirteen

Maximise Energy

Being D.E.A.R. to Yourself

Diet **E**xercise **A**ttitude **R**est

maximise: *increase to the greatest possible amount or degree.*

energy: *the capacity for vigorous activity; available power;*
an adequate or abundant amount of such power;
the ability to act, lead others, effect, etc, forcefully.
vitality of action or expression.

People who thrive have boundless energy to pursue their dreams and goals. They have the physical and mental energy to do whatever they need to do to succeed. They are definitely not the people who are 'too tired' or 'can't be bothered' to do the work required to achieve their goals. They have the mental and physical energy to develop a project, take on a challenge, get the grades, build a business, have fun with their partner and children, reach the pinnacle in their chosen career path and do the work required to succeed in their field of endeavour. I use the word energy to indicate that vital, enthusiastic aura that is evident in those who succeed in realising their potential. Don't we all want the energy to do what it takes to achieve our dreams and goals?

It's vital that we all know how to look after our health and wellbeing: understand that prevention is better than cure. It is also essential, if we are to realise our goals and perform at our best when it matters most, that we understand how to maintain and maximise our energy levels.

Energy gives us vitality, enables us to pursue our passions and, for the most part, is something entirely within our control. Energy is essential to achieve what we want in life. It obviously links to being healthy, but energy is more than health and makes all the difference in our capacity to succeed. There are people who are healthy but still do not feel energised or radiate energy. On the other hand, there are individuals who overcome massive physical and health challenges and still demonstrate incredible energy, such as the Stephen Hawking, a theoretical physicist, cosmologist, author of a number of books, including the best seller, *A Brief History of Time: From Big Bang To Black Hole*, and ex Director of Research at the Centre for Theoretical Cosmology within the University of Cambridge, and all with motor neurone disease.

Maximising our energy levels has clear links with being able to harness the enormous power of passion and positivity. It's a key factor in being able to 'do the work' required to achieve our goals. Each milestone along the way takes energy, from engaging the right people to help us to spending all weekend packing the boxes to ship out for our fledgling on-line shoe business, from studying long hours for an examination, to doing the punishing training regime required to perform at our best in elite sport, dance or music. Energy not only enables us to physically do what we need to, but it's vital if we're going to harness all the power of our brain to learn, create and achieve our goals.

I believe that there are four essential elements to ensuring we have maximum energy, and I created the acronym **D.E.A.R.** to help us remember these and focus on the fact that having energy means looking after ourselves: body and mind. Wellbeing and energy are synonymous, for me, and to achieve both we need to be D.E.A.R. to ourselves and get the balance right in our:

Diet   **E**xercise   **A**ttitude   **R**est

Before we look at what being **D.E.A.R.** to ourselves means, let's just remind ourselves about maintaining positive habits.

Habits

Maximising our energy, health and wellbeing
is all about developing
informed, positive habits to appropriately balance our
Diet Exercise Attitude Rest

Both positive and negative habits are developed from birth, and we can maintain or change them throughout our lives. Some of us develop habits very quickly, and some of us take a long time to establish them. All of us take a while to change our them. Our habits also need to be constantly challenged and re-informed if we are to have the wherewithal to achieve and maintain our wellbeing. Being D.E.A.R. to ourselves is all about developing those essential positive habits to look after ourselves and maximise our energy.

 Being D.E.A.R. to Ourselves

Below are some thoughts about how we can be D.E.A.R. to ourselves, maximise our energy levels and enable our children to maintain the right balance of diet, exercise, attitude and rest. I am deeply grateful to my daughter, Harriet, for being my expert guide for this chapter with her deep knowledge and understanding of exercise and nutrition.

Diet

Basically, eating and drinking healthily is vital for our mental and physical wellbeing, and a major contributor to maintaining our energy levels. It is important for us to understand what nutrients we need to stay healthy and have maximum energy when we need it most. We also need to know which foods make us sluggish and lethargic and avoid them. Let's also not forget the importance of water; our brain utilises 75-80% of our total water intake and therefore water is vital if we're to keep performing at our best, physically and mentally.

The key with nutrition, like exercise, is to get into a regular routine to avoid spikes and troughs in our energy levels due to what we eat or drink. Things high in sugary carbohydrates, such as sweet foods and sugary drinks, are a quick fix, but they will cause energy levels to quickly dip lower than they were originally. Simply, if we maintain a healthy balance of carbohydrate, protein, fat, vitamins and minerals we will feel great and full of energy. It's about doing some research and choosing the foods that suit us.

Food Groups

Some nutrients provide energy, while others are essential for growth and maintenance of the body. Carbohydrate, protein and fat are macronutrients that we need to eat in relatively large amounts as they provide our bodies with energy, and are also the building blocks for growth and maintenance of a healthy body. Vitamins and minerals are micronutrients which are only needed in small amounts, but are essential to keep us healthy. There are also some food components that are not strictly 'nutrients', but are important for health, such as water and fibre. As a reminder, there is an overview of food groups with examples on the equipped2succeed website.

Carbohydrates

We know we need some carbohydrate in our diets, however this should not take over; it's about quality. Too many of us eat more carbohydrates than we need. White bread isn't going to provide you with anywhere near as much energy as wholegrain. The same goes for pasta, rice, and so on. As with everything, balance is key.

Protein

It's not only carbohydrates that provide us with energy, protein also plays a key role in boosting our energy levels. Protein is primarily for repair in the body, repairing all bodily tissues vital to keep us healthy and developing. The best way to get all the essential proteins we need is to ensure we eat a good balance of fish, meat and plant sources, such as beans and pulses.

Fats

Despite our obsession with low fat, fat is an essential part of a healthy diet if eaten in moderation. There are, however, different fats, some of which have a positive effect and some of which have a negative effect on our bodies. The best way is to get the fats we need from natural, unprocessed fats, such as avocado, nuts and fish, and not pastries, cakes and fried food where the fat has been processed so heavily that our bodies are unable to digest it effectively.

Vitamins and Minerals

Vitamins and minerals are a small proportion of our diet that have a big impact. We can't store most vitamins and minerals. We therefore need to ensure that we eat them every day, the best sources being fresh vegetables, especially green vegetables, salads and fruit.

'Superfoods'

'Superfoods' are increasingly promoted and many have been scientifically proven to boost energy as well as providing a whole host of other health benefits. One of the latest mainstream treatments for prostrate cancer is a tablet containing totally natural ingredients including some superfoods; broccoli, pomegranate and turmeric spice. The initial trials have shown a dramatic impact on reducing cancer in those with low-level prostrate cancer. To confirm the importance of these foods, we only have to look at the selection of books on this subject, and search the web to find numerous articles about all the range of health promoting foods that are available to us, along with the benefits they provide.

Keeping it simple

There are a few simple things that we can do in order to ensure that we keep our diets on track for energy and vitality without making it unduly complicated.

Keep it Fresh

Primarily, we are animals, and it isn't until relatively recently that we have forced our bodies to consume and digest all kinds of processed foods. Most of us have a favourite fast food and have picked up a quick ready meal on the way home from work. But our bodies just don't like it. We've spent thousands of years eating what we could from our environment: fresh, organic food. This is what our bodies are used to and this is what our bodies respond best to. It's easier to digest unprocessed food, meaning our bodies can make efficient use of all the nutrients it provides. By avoiding processed foods, we also minimise the additives and toxins that we introduce into our bodies, and more importantly, into our children's bodies.

In terms of recognising processed food, the basic general rule is to look at the list of ingredients:

Long list of ingredients = BAD
Example: a brand of one pot dried meal:
'Noodles, Wheat Flour, Vegetable Oil, Firming Agents – Potassium Carbonate, Sodium Carbonate, Water, Vegetables – Carrot, Onion, Peas, Maltodexin (which I assume is a version of maltodextrin), Sugar, Flavourings, Cheese Powder, Low Sodium Mineral Salt (Contains Potassium), Acidity Regulator (Sodium Diacetate), Flavour Enhancer (Monosodium Glutamate), Yeast Extract, Curry Powder, Ground Cumin, Spice Extracts, Chilli Powder, Mango Chutney Sauce (Sugar, Mangos, Salt, Acetic Acid, Spices), Water, Spirit Vinegar, Modified Maize Starch. May Contain Soya.'

Long list of ingredients you don't recognise and with lots of numbers = VERY BAD
Example: a brand of sweets:
'Dextrose, Sugar, Malic Acid, Corn Syrup*. Artificial Flavours: Carnauba Wax. Artificial Colours: Brilliant Blue (E133)**, Allura Red (E129)**, Tartrazine (E102)**.
** This may have an adverse effect on activity and attention in children.
Allegan Information: Contains Egg, *May contain GMO (which stands for genetically modified organisms).'

Short list of ingredients – BETTER
Example: a well-known brand of tinned tomato soup:

'Tomatoes, Water, Vegetable Oil, Sugar, Modified Cornflour, Salt, Dried Skimmed Milk, Milk Proteins, Cream, Spice Extracts, Herb Extract, Citric Acid.
No artificial colours. No artificial flavours. No artificial preservatives.'

NB – the lists of ingredients above are copied directly from food packaging. The only bits I've added are explanations in italics.

No list of ingredients - BEST
Example: there are no lists on fresh food: fresh fruit, fresh vegetables, fresh fish, fresh meat, dried herbs and spices, home-made food.

We do best if we can avoid foods with lists of ingredients that contain sugar, especially as a main ingredient (often used in low-fat foods to enhance taste), artificial flavouring, artificial colours, numbers; and remember:

If it doesn't tell you how many calories,
you know it's better nutrition.

I recognise that we have always needed to preserve things, especially before the times of freezing or the importation out-of-season vegetables and fruits, but there are more natural ways of doing this.

Variety
Another important factor is variety. An apple a day may or may not keep the doctor away, but realistically, we need far more variety than this. If we're not sure when it comes to fruit and vegetables, the best way to ensure we get what we need is to go for as many colours as possible. This will ensure we get all the vitamins and minerals we need, not forgetting those all-important anti-oxidants, which, amongst their many benefits, reduce wrinkles and ageing. So, even for those odd moments when we are not feeling particularly energised, at least we'll look like we are.

'Kiddie Food' – To Be Avoided

Food designed and marketed especially for children is a relatively new invention, and tends to be the ultimate processed food, coloured, pummelled and packaged to attract little people and full of sugar and salt. Examples include the standard kiddie menu fare in cafes of chicken nuggets, fish fingers, burgers, and so on. Isn't it more healthy for our children to be eating fresh, unprocessed food containing as few additives and toxins as possible?

Portion Size

Sometimes, many of us all struggle is portion size. It's not too bold a statement to say most of us eat more than we need to be healthy. How much should we eat? How much should we put on our plates? How much food should we put on our children's plates or encourage them to put on their own plates as they grow?

I remember when I was young my father being very against forcing children to eat everything that was on their plate, which was not in line with the prevailing attitude of the time in a small Derbyshire village. He said that forcing people to eat food they didn't want or need was worse than throwing it away. Don't get me wrong, he also didn't agree with snacking between meals, so we couldn't get away with not eating our meal then snacking instead. He also told us what his Uncle Albert had told him, *'Always stop eating when you could eat just a little bit more'*. Sounds more like current diet advice than wisdom from a farming community in the 1930s!

I am constantly reviewing my diet, as I think we all need to do periodically as we age, our lifestyles change and we look to prevent health issues in natural ways. At one point I saw an Ayurveda practitioner. One exercise she carried out with me on portion size was very powerful. She started by saying that nature has a very good way of telling us how much we should eat. She then asked me to hold my hands together and poured dried red kidney beans into my hands until they were about to overflow. The size of our meal should be no more than we can hold in our hands. If we are a different size, it makes sense that we need different amounts of food and what we can hold in our hands is a great, natural way of seeing that. How many of us only eat that amount of food at a meal?

Energy Boosts

Energy drinks can be very misleading. Some people think that caffeine-filled energy drinks are an acceptable way to boost energy. They can give us a short-lived energy boost but, as well as being full of sugar, can cause poor attention, make us intolerant, anxious and quick to anger.

Drinks with high levels of caffeine that can become addictive. The energy they produce also only lasts a short period of time, and then needs replenishing, which means we are more likely to become dependent on the caffeine for energy. Before we know it, we're stuck in a vicious cycle which is difficult to break. In addition, we've got the issue of caffeine being a drug, so once we stop drinking it we feel awful. It can often cause headaches and feelings of extreme tiredness.

Sports drinks are a growing trend as an every day drink, rather than only when we're participating in sports. There are two main types: hypertonic and hypotonic. The glucose concentration in a hypertonic drink is higher than the concentration in the blood resulting in quick absorption of glucose into the blood, therefore providing an increase in energy levels. However, hypertonic drinks are not the most effective for hydration. Hypotonic drinks contain less glucose concentration than the blood. The body, therefore, absorbs more water resulting in increased hydration.

The Power of Water

And, of course, there's always plain water, which we know is vital for our bodies in so many ways. The value of water is mentioned in many chapters of this book. How many of us are drinking the recommended two litres a day for adults?

In day-to-day life, we just need plain water. With aerobic exercise, we need a mix of drinks. If you've ever watched Wimbledon (or any tennis tournament), you might have noticed that all tennis players have two or three bottles, which they drink from between games or sets. This is to ensure that they get a mix of hypertonic and hypotonic drinks, as well as water.

If we're sitting at our desk all day, there is no reason why we need a drink high in sugar or caffeine. If we have a healthy diet, all we need is water. **Our brains utilise 75%-80% of the water we drink, and if our brains are working effectively, then so are we**. I do, however, recognise the difference between 'need' and 'want', and sometimes a little of what we want serves a need that isn't strictly nutritional. That is fine if we're conscious of the fact it is a want, rather than a need, we are fulfilling, and there are minimal harmful effects.

Key themes:

> **Keep It Fresh**: as much as possible, eat just fresh food, which naturally avoids the damaging toxins, sugars, fats and salt that is in all processed food.
> **Balance**: ensure we're eating food from all the food groups in the right proportion. If we have a mix of colours from natural food sources on our plate, we're not far off!
> Remember Uncle Albert's advice, *'Stop eating when you could eat just a little bit more'.*

> **Drink Water**

> **Find What Suits You**

 Exercise

Regular exercise or physical activity is a vital ingredient to maintaining and increasing our energy levels, enabling us to do what it takes to pursue our goals.

Over thousands of years, our bodies have developed to move. Our bodies like movement. Movement is natural to us and it helps keep our bodies and minds healthy. Exercise is good for us. Period.

Exercise improves our oxygen intake, and the efficiency with which our organs and bodily tissues can use that oxygen, resulting in us being able to function better. It is essential for physical, mental and emotional health. When you consider that 21% of the air we breath is made up of oxygen, and out of that 21% we breath out 16%, we really need to make the most of the remaining 5%. 20-25% of our oxygen intake is used by the brain, which is even more reason to increase the amount of oxygen we take in and use it effectively. Exercise is the best way to do this.

Physical activity is essential to maintain our mental, as well as physical, wellbeing. Most of us don't do manual labour, and many of us are in sedentary jobs, that are internally stressful and physically passive, which is the worst combination in maintaining our health, wellbeing and vitality, as well as our energy levels. It is therefore crucial that we find exercise that we enjoy to develop and maintain our holistic wellbeing.

Exercise means something different to everyone. For one person walking the dog is their work out, whereas others may need to 'get a sweat on' in the gym to feel like they've done some beneficial exercise. The key is to find the level that suits you. If your heart rate is raised and you get a bit out of breath, then that's exercise, whatever form it may take. There's also exercise, like yoga, that specifically links mind and body, and is good for strength and suppleness.

If we are going to maintain our exercise regime, we are probably going to need to enjoy it. Our time is precious. If it doesn't come naturally to us, finding something we enjoy and doing it with a friend is the best way to establish the habit. If we enjoy the activity, recognise the benefits, make it social and enjoy the environment, we are much more likely to maintain it. If we feel awkward and uncomfortable in a gym, we won't go and won't enjoy it when we do.

It's helpful to try alternative exercise or sports that we can do at varying venues and environments to find what we enjoy. When it comes to choosing exercise, the key is just to have a go and not be put off if our first experience of exercise is challenging. There is so much available, from parks where we can set ourselves little challenges to add fun and fitness to a walk, great family fitness activities which work for busy parents, and a plethora of 'new' sports or dance activities, as well as the ones we all know. Local neighbourhood or regional websites have lots of information and the governing bodies of the various sports give information on where we can join in locally. Being part of a group can help the enjoyment and motivation to use our bodies.

Basically, if we find some form of exercise following which we feel makes us satisfied, after we've done it, and mentally energised or calmed, then we've found what works for us. The sooner we get into the habit of exercising regularly, the better. If you eat a pack of sweets with 'e' numbers, or drink a pot of strong coffee, you will get an almost instantaneous burst of energy. But it doesn't last! You go for an early morning walk and feel energised and refreshed for the rest of the day.

We've all heard of endorphins, known as 'happy hormones', which are released in the body when exercising. Current research suggests that, in order to get the additional release of endorphins, you need to exercise at a high intensity: putting your body in a state of stress where there is insufficient oxygen to meet the demands of the body. This isn't to say that there is no benefit from low-intensity exercise. There is major benefit. However, to get the true 'runner's high', you need to train hard. Endorphins are released whenever the body is put under emotional or physical stress, so if you jump out of a plane, you will get a huge boost of endorphins; if you really push yourself out of your comfort zone and speak to an audience of a thousand people, it has the same effect. For most of us, it seems much easier to work up a sweat in the park to get that good feeling! It is with exercise as it is with everything:

Those who want to do something find a way; those who don't find an excuse.

 Attitude

You Get Out What You Put In.

Positive emotional energy is the key to health, happiness and wellbeing. The more positive you are, the better your life will be in every area.
Brian Tracy

Our attitude has a big impact on our energy levels. Successful people can keep going when others may be feeling tired, and this has a lot to do with their positive mental attitude. A positive attitude and approach is crucial to maintaining enthusiasm and high energy. The importance of a positive attitude is explored in Chapter seven; *Be Positive*, so I am only highlighting a few things specifically linked to energy in this section. The power of the mind is incredible in enabling us to gather the energy we need to do the things that are important to us: for example when we say that we are tired, then we will think that we are tired, so we will be tired. Having goals we are passionate about and staying positive and focused on achieving our goals helps us maintain the energy we need for gruelling training programmes, essential study, and long meetings into the night.

Others reflect back to us our energy and positivity. It's therefore vital that we are energy givers rather than energy sappers. We've all met them, and I'm sure you can think of the people in your life who give you energy and those who sap it – if you allow them to. It's what you might call a virtuous cycle. Positive words and a smiling face can give energy to us, and those around us. They then reflect that energy back to us in a smile, a gesture or positive words that give us even more energy. You can see the impact of this en masse in a sports stadium when the mass energy of fans gives the team extra impetus.

Try smiling more, at home, at work, in the supermarket; you'll be amazed at the results! Laughter is also proven to boost positive endorphins and energy, so it's important to laugh: to find humour and use humour for our own benefit and the benefit of those around us. By humour, I don't mean the negative, put-down, sarcastic type that can belittle and sap energy, but the kind that makes us all chuckle.

Laughter is the sun that drives winter
from the human face.
Victor Hugo

We have all had times when we've not had enough rest, but enthusiasm and desire fuel us to pursue things we are passionate about. We don't let our babies cry in the middle of the night because we're too tired; we don't miss important deadlines because we're too tired; we don't let friends down because we're too tired; we don't let our team down because we're too tired. There's a saying in sport, 'Leave it all on the field', which means give every last bit of physical and mental energy you've got to obtain the result you desire. Those who succeed in anything find the energy to go that extra step, dig deep and find a bit more when others are only prepared to work well within their physical and mental limits. This applies in anything: doing the work necessary to achieve the grades you want in exams; successfully completing a project; starting a business; making that important breakthrough in science, IT, engineering; becoming elite in sport, music, dance or any area of the arts.

This, the last of human freedoms; to choose one's attitude in
any given set of circumstances, to choose one's own way.
Victor Frankl

Maintaining a positive attitude and energy includes not allowing others' negativity to drain our energy levels. We need to surround ourselves with positive people who help us maintain our energy levels and help our children to do the same.

How we think we feel has a definite effect on how we actually
feel physically. If your mind tells you that you are tired, the
body mechanism, the nerves, and the muscles accept the fact.
If your mind is intensely interested,
you can keep on at an activity indefinitely.
Norman Vincent Peale

 # Rest

The best bridge between despair and hope is a
good night's sleep.
E. Joseph Cossman

What do we mean by rest? Rest can be both sleep and relaxation, or just changing our routine. Most of us need an average of seven or eight hours sleep a night to maintain our energy levels and be at our best when we need it most. Parents soon see what sleep deprivation does when we have children. In simple terms, tiredness prevents us from being at our best. We learn to mask tiredness as we get older, but it is no coincidence that a quick nap is called a 'power nap'. Many successful people use short naps to top-up their energy levels at key times, for example, just before an important presentation or meeting, or just before a sporting performance. Athletes plan their essential rest times into their training programme. It doesn't need to be for a long period of time to benefit us. Ellen McArthur, the round the world sailor, and Richard Branson are great examples of what a power nap can do for us!

Appropriate sleep and rest contributes to:
- mental alertness
- ability to handle stress
- good memory
- ability to concentrate
- healthy appetite with appropriate portion size
- best use of our eyes
- best use of our motor skills
- ability to manage relationships
- health and vitality
- ability to be calm and measured in our approach

Lack of sleep contributes to:
- fuzzy thinking
- inability to handle stress
- poor memory
- inability to concentrate

- increased appetite
- vision problems
- poor decision making
- diminished motor skills
- relationship troubles
- medical problems
- mood swings

 Think about what impact this may have at every stage of our lives in:

- school
- work
- relationships

Think about what impact this may have in pressured situations; such as:

- examinations
- trials
- sports performances
- music exams
- driving tests
- interviews
- pitches
- presentations

According to the Royal College of Psychiatrists, at any given time, one in five people feels unusually tired, and one in ten have prolonged fatigue. Women tend to feel tired more than men. Tiredness that is not linked to lack of rest or genuine physical tiredness can mean that we don't sleep well, which can turn into a vicious circle. Most of the time, fatigue is linked with mood and the accumulation of lots of little stresses in life. Physical activity or exercise gives us the 'good' physical tiredness that helps us rest well. It can help to ensure that our caffeine intake isn't keeping us from high quality rest. Using relaxation techniques to calm our minds also helps us rest well.

Our sleep patterns are dictated by light and hormones. When light dims in the evening, we produce a chemical called melatonin, which gives the body clock its cue, telling us it's time to sleep. *'The problem is that society has changed,'* says Dr. Paul Gringras, director of the Evelina Paediatric Sleep Disorder Service at Guy's and St Thomas' Hospital in London. *'Artificial light has disrupted our sleep patterns. Bright room lighting, TVs, games consoles and PCs can all emit enough light to stop the natural production of melatonin.'* Other distractions include mobile phones and instant messaging, which many of us may use well into the night.

The clear message is that we need to be mindful of this and do all we can to avoid the communication and stimulation overload that can have such detrimental affects on our sleep patterns. We also owe it to ourselves to ensure that we have a diet and exercise regime that allows us to develop and maintain healthy patterns of rest.

Being D.E.A.R. to ourselves is a lifestyle choice we can all implement. We can all develop and maintain these positive habits and have the health, wellbeing and vitality to do what's important for us.

Affirmations
- *I am feeling great; maintaining the physical and mental energy for everything I want to do.*
- *I am exercising regularly and feeling energised.*
- *I am eating and drinking to maintain my health.*
- *I am maximising my mental and physical energy.*
- *I am positive and have boundless for what's important to me.*

 ACTION

1. One of the things we can do to check that we're maximising our energy is to keep an **Energy Diary** for a couple of weeks: something very simple, so it's easy to maintain. It will help us to recognise the positive and negative benefits of certain things and help us learn how best to maintain our energy balance. Complete it three times a day, at the same times each day, as far as possible. Use a simple table to include these headings:

Day................. Time.......... Time.......... Time..........

Eat

Drink

Exercise

Rest

Attitude

Energy Level (score out of 10)

2. Use the Energy Diary to check when your energy levels are at their highest, and when they dip, and reflect:
High Energy or Low Energy
Why?
Which of the four key factors was in or out of balance in the last 24 hours?
Did you eat energy-giving foods? Or foods that make you lethargic?
Have you drunk plenty of water?
Did you do any physical activity/exercise?
Did you rest enough?
What was your attitude like?
What was the attitude of those around you like?
Are you remaining positive?

Are you allowing others to give you energy or drain your energy?

Once we are in tune with our energy levels and the reasons for energy dips, we find it much easier to maintain high energy.

3. Set a goal and action plan to increase your energy levels or maintain high energy.
   When setting your goal and creating your action plan, think about the four key elements to developing and maintaining high energy and decide what the priorities are for you.

4. Encourage your children to try new foods – turn it into a game of deciding what it tastes like, looks like and so on.

I'm into wellbeing, not because of social pressures to look a certain way, but because I'm interested in living a long, full and healthy life.
Kelly Brook

Sufficient sleep, exercise, healthy food, friendship, and peace of mind are necessities, not luxuries.
Mark Halperin

Chapter Fourteen

Getting On Well With People

Bringing out the best in ourselves and others

The most important single ingredient in the formula of success is knowing how to get along with people.
Theodore Roosevelt

manage: *to bring about or succeed in accomplishing;*
to influence;
to handle, direct, govern, or control.

relationships: *a connection, association, or involvement;*
emotional or other connection between people;
the way in which two or more people or groups regard and behave towards each other.

To achieve success in all areas of our life, we need to understand ourselves, manage ourselves effectively, and form effective relationships with those around us.

The title of this chapter ought to be *Manage Ourselves Well, Our Emotions and Behaviour, Individually and Within Relationships,* but of course that's far too long! However, it's a far more accurate description of what we are consistently working on. We can learn to effectively play our part in relationships and we can influence others, but just as we can't manage time, we can't really manage relationships. What we can do is learn to manage ourselves, and tune in to, and influence others.

In personal relationships, social situations and most work situations, it is vital to recognise how important it is to understand ourselves and manage ourselves effectively in order to achieve the best outcomes. This is especially true when it matters most: being a good friend when we're really needed; in those differences with friends; in that all-important interview; playing our role in the team; leading our team; and behaving appropriately in those important and challenging personal, social and work situations. Successful people realise how important it is to manage themselves effectively and get on well with others: forming positive relationships and behaving appropriately to bring about beneficial outcomes. They are also aware of the power of emotions and they reflect on their behaviour with others.

In my view, there are three essential elements to managing yourself effectively and managing relationships for the benefit of all:

Emotional Literacy: understanding emotional intelligence and constantly improving our emotional literacy;

Being Assertive: understanding the importance of assertive behaviour and developing our capacity to be assertive, rather than passive or aggressive, to develop healthy relationships;

Teamwork: understanding the essentials of teamwork and learning how best to contribute to, and lead, teams.

These are interlinked and the common denominator is communication in all its forms. There are obviously some specific fields of endeavour where relationships with people are exceptionally important, and those where they are less so. If we start a retail business, for example, we have many relationships that we need to effectively manage and be good at: to gain support from those from whom we require help to set up; customers; employees; suppliers; premises landlord; the list is endless. Even if your performance and success is less people-focused, such as scientific research and individual pursuits, we all need to engage with and elicit support from people at some point, and it is always helpful if those relationships are positive.

The People Stuff Is Important!

If your emotional abilities aren't in hand, if you don't have self-awareness, if you are not able to manage your distressing emotions, if you can't have empathy and have effective relationships, then no matter how smart you are, you are not going to get very far.
Daniel Goleman

Those people who thrive know themselves: are aware of their emotional temperature and are able to manage their internal states. They develop themselves to become comfortable in most situations, and collaborate with people who complement their strengths. They are able to 'tune in' to the people they meet, at work and socially, through interpersonal skills and 'doing their homework': finding out what's important to others. Emotional literacy, social literacy and assertiveness are not systematically developed in many school curricula. We are expected to pick-up these behaviours by some form of social osmosis. If we don't, by the time we're adults, very few people are going to point out short comings in our interpersonal skills but they will limit us. It is therefore important for us to recognise and develop these capabilities for ourselves.

This chapter focuses on the three things that I regard as the most essential aspects of knowing yourself and getting on well with those around you. If we know ourselves and can tune into and manage our emotional state, we can reflect accurately on our behaviour and modify it according to the situation. If we get on well with others, and can manage relationships effectively in all contexts, we reap the rewards in so many ways. I am still learning, and still get things wrong, by saying the wrong thing at the wrong time in the wrong way, as we all do, but the important thing is that we are aware when we get things wrong and what to do about it.

In all aspects of managing ourselves effectively with others, for me, there are the Three Rs:

Respect:

Treat everyone as an individual and respect them as individuals, both their micro and macro culture:

- o micro culture: their home, their way of doing things, what they can do rather than what they can't;
- o macro culture: in society, their contribution, their heritage, their customs, their religion.

Reflect:

It is only by systematic reflection that we learn the complexities of getting on well with people in all sorts of contexts and learn to amend our behaviour according to the situation. In this way, we learn from situations where we've handled things well and where we could have handled things better.

Review:

Make changes; amend our behaviour as we grow and learn. 'I'm just like that' is not acceptable if our behaviour stands in the way of us having mutually affirming, rewarding and beneficial relationships.

Pretend that every single person you meet has a sign around his or her neck that says, 'Make me feel important.
Mary Kay Ash

Constant And Never-ending Improvement applies in relationships, as with anything else. If we are always learning, we have the capacity to make our personal, social and professional relationships richer all the time. The alternative is not learning, growing or adapting, and then our relationships are likely to become more impoverished and continuously challenging.

Emotions and Behaviour

How well we interact with others boils down to **emotions** and **behaviour**:

- what we feel;
- what others feel;
- what we say and how we say it;
- what others say and how they say it;

- how we receive what others say. How we feel and how we respond;
- what we do and how we do it;
- what others do and how they do it;
- how we receive what others do. How we feel and how we respond.

Just looking at this list gives us an insight into the complexity of managing ourselves and managing relationships effectively. If we add into that mix how we need to amend our language and behaviour according to the context, the mix gets more complex.

Nothing is perfect. Life is messy. Relationships are complex. Outcomes are uncertain. People are irrational.
Hugh Mackay

Being aware, reflecting and reviewing, and continuously learning, enables us to make the most of relationships with others. This chapter focuses on:

- managing ourselves;
- being consistently more assertive;
- bringing out the best in ourselves and others;
- participating in, and leading, teams.

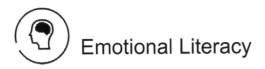 # Emotional Literacy

Anyone can become angry – that is easy. But to be angry with the right person, to the right degree, at the right time, for the right purpose, and in the right way – this is not easy.
Aristotle

Emotional literacy enables us to be self-aware and to accurately self-reflect: constantly improve our ability to manage ourselves, and improve our interactions and behaviour with people. We need to understand ourselves, be positive with ourselves, and behave appropriately and positively with others to achieve successful relationships in all areas of our life: with family, with friends, in work, anywhere we need to get on with people, and that's pretty much everywhere! Developing emotional literacy is about understanding emotional intelligence and becoming more competent in managing our emotions.

What is Emotional Intelligence?

Much of our current understanding of emotional intelligence has come from Daniel Goleman's work.   Daniel Goleman is an internationally-renowned psychologist whose 1995 book, *Emotional Intelligence – Why it Can Matter More Than IQ,* was on *The New York Times* bestseller list for eighteen months, with more than five million copies in print worldwide in forty languages. He has written a number of further books expanding our whole understanding of the way we manage our emotional state and effectively relate to others. His books, *Working with Emotional Intelligence* and *The New Leaders – transforming the Art of Leadership into the science of Results* with Richard Boyatzis and Annie McKee, have had a major impact worldwide on our view of effective management and leadership, and how leadership has needed to change to meet the demands of our changing economic and social environment. Daniel Goleman's work has enabled me to put what I have learned from experience into context. It gives a clear framework to help us reflect on, and develop, our emotional literacy.

Daniel Goleman's **Emotional Competence Framework** from *Working with Emotional Intelligence* is broken down into personal and social competencies. It is one of the most comprehensive, straightforward frameworks for reflecting and developing our emotional literacy and competence.

Personal Competence
These competencies determine how we mange ourselves.

Self-Awareness
Knowing our internal states or emotional temperature, our preferences, our personal resources, and our intuitions.

Emotional awareness: recognising our emotions and their effects on others.

Accurate self-assessment: knowing our strengths and where we need to improve.

Self-confidence: a strong sense of our self-worth and capabilities.

Being self-aware is vital if we are to recognise and understand our feelings and trust the accuracy of their interpretation. This is the fundamental building block for us to be equipped to effectively manage ourselves, and our relationships with others. Accurate self-reflection is a vital tool for improvement in any area, and it is the most valuable tool when it comes to managing our emotional state and behaviour.

Self-Regulation

Managing our internal states or emotions, our impulses, and our personal resources.

Self-Control: keeping disruptive, negative emotions and impulses in check.

Trustworthiness: maintaining standards of honesty and integrity.

Conscientiousness: taking responsibility for a high standard of personal performance.

Adaptability: flexibility in handling change.

Innovation: being comfortable with innovative ideas, approaches, and new information.

Regulating ourselves, taking control and managing our emotions, is one of the most challenging aspects of emotional literacy. Breathing deeply and reflecting, taking that moment to consider our response and responding appropriately, especially in difficult situations, is something most of us find challenging. It is essential to develop this competence to engage effectively with others.

Anger is never without a reason, but seldom a good one.
Benjamin Franklin

Motivation

Emotional tendencies that guide or facilitate reaching our goals.

> **Achievement drive:** striving to improve or meet a standard of excellence.
> **Commitment:** aligning our goals with the goals of the groups or organisations of which we are members.
> **Initiative:** readiness to act on opportunities.
> **Optimism:** persistence in pursuing goals despite obstacles and setbacks.

This summarises the 'get up and go' required to consistently move forward with whatever we are pursuing. It also emphasises how we need to 'tune in to' the environment and people around us, personally, socially, and in our chosen fields of endeavour.

Social Competence

These competencies determine how we handle relationships.

Empathy

Awareness of others' feelings, needs and concerns.

> *Empathy is one of the essential traits we need to challenge stereotypes and overcome prejudices.*
> Roman Krznaric

> **Understanding others:** sensing others' feelings and perspectives, and taking an active interest in their concerns.
> **Developing others:** sensing others' development needs and bolstering their abilities.
> **Service orientation:** anticipating, recognising, and meeting customers' needs.
> **Leveraging diversity:** cultivating opportunities through different kinds of people.
> **Political awareness:** reading a group's emotional currents and power relationships.

*Everything that irritates us about others can
lead us to an understanding of ourselves.*
Carl Gustav Jung

Social Skills
Adeptness at responding appropriately to others and
bringing about desirable responses in others.

>**Influence:** wielding effective tactics for persuasion.
>**Communication:** listening openly and sending convincing
>messages.
>**Conflict management:** negotiating and resolving
>disagreements.
>**Leadership:** inspiring and guiding individuals and groups.
>**Change catalyst:** initiating or managing change.
>**Building bonds:** nurturing mutually helpful relationships.
>**Collaboration and co-operation:** working with others
>towards shared goals.
>**Team capabilities:** creating group synergy in pursuing
>collective goals.

*I will not waste my life in friction when it could be
turned into momentum.*
Frances Willard

Most of us constantly strive to improve our social skills from a young age, realising the importance of being happy in our personal relationships, feeling comfortable and enjoying fulfilling relationships in all areas of our life. We also recognise how vital our social competency is to gaining the help we need to achieve our goals. However, we all know people who are skilled and knowledgeable in all sorts of ways, but who are uncomfortable with people, show little empathy, fail to pick up social cues on behaviour and fail to engage appropriately in social and work situations. They miss out on realising their potential. They have technical ability and experience, but haven't gained those essential people skills that enable them to use their expertise to best effect.

There is a commonly-held belief that we learn these competencies and skills by 'osmosis'. We pick them up along the way and if we don't, it's held against us as some personal flaw, or those around us just say, 's/he's just like that'. Daniel Goleman's, and others', research, our own experience of the changing, complex nature of social interaction and the working environment, clearly point to the fact that this is not enough.

The fact that many of us now work in smaller organisations, where it's even more important that we get on with our colleagues, adds to the importance of this. The main challenge we have in making this explicit within the education and training curricula is that emotional intelligence cannot be taught like facts and knowledge beyond the basic framework. Personal and social competencies are mainly learned through a coaching and experiential learning approach to education and training. This involves sharing essential understanding and tools, and reflecting on, and exploring, real-life experiences and scenarios. It is therefore largely down to us to develop the essential competencies we need to manage ourselves and manage our many and varied relationships.

> *For every minute you remain angry, you give up*
> *sixty seconds of peace of mind. (Or happiness!)*
> Ralph Waldo Emerson

To paraphrase Aristotle, challenging the right person, to the right degree, at the right time, for the right purpose, and in the right way is challenging and it's down to us to continuously reflect, learn and improve.

 # Being Assertive

The aim of assertive behaviour is to communicate productively
with another person, achieving what is often described as
a win-win outcome.

Being assertive is an aspect of emotional competence, and an important part of equipping ourselves to effectively engage in mutually beneficial relationships, expressing our thoughts and feelings in an appropriate way, and standing up for ourselves. From my experience, I think many of the behaviour issues and confrontations that arise in people's interactions could be avoided if we were all more assertive. Over the years, I have used a wide variety of sources to help me put together workshops that enable individuals to improve their capacity to assert themselves. In this section, I share a few of the insights that have guided my approach.

Assertive People Believe they have the Right to:
- have their own values, beliefs, opinions, and emotions;
- tell others how they wish to be treated;
- express themselves and say, 'No,' 'I don't know,' 'I don't understand';
- take the time they need to formulate their ideas before expressing them;
- make mistakes;
- stand up for themselves and for what they believe and want;
- be treated with respect.

Many assertive people also do not feel compelled to justify or explain their actions to others, and may become irritated at having to do this, even when it's appropriate to do so! This may be a positive or negative according to the context and your perspective. However, when challenged, the assertive person will explain themselves clearly and without the negative traits of defensiveness or aggression.

Behaving Assertively
To behave assertively we need to pay attention to our eye contact, tone of voice and body language, as well as the words we use. There are variations on eye contact and body language, according to culture, so we all need to remember to check cultural norms when we are travelling.

DIRECT EYE-CONTACT

CALM CLEAR TONE OF VOICE

OPEN BODY LANGUAGE

CAREFULLY CHOOSING THE WORDS YOU USE

The Four Behaviour Types

It is generally recognised that there are four main ways of behaving: passive, aggressive, passive/aggressive and assertive. The following table provides a summary of the four behaviour types and the behaviour, voice, speech pattern, facial expressions, eye contact and body language we associate with them.

Most of us behave in all these ways at some time (or 'milder' versions of them), often behaving differently in different situations, but we can all change and continuously develop our assertive behaviour to improve our relationships. We can also enable our children to develop assertive behaviour by teaching them about society's norms and expectations, and about the elements of assertive behaviour. We can reflect back to them the way they've said things and how that makes us feel, or might make someone else feel, coaching them in appropriate responses and how they should ask for what they want in an appropriate manner.

Behaviour Type	Voice	Speech Pattern	Face	Body Language	Actions
Passive Keen to avoid confrontation, often by suppressing their own needs; hopes people will 'know' what he or she wants; excessively concerned with what other people think of him or her.	Sometimes 'wobbly'. Tone may be whining. Very soft, quiet or childlike. Often dull or monotonous. Drops away at the end of a sentence.	Hesitant, many pauses. May stress 'you' words. Frequent throat-clearing. Gives up when interrupted.	Feint, false smiles when expressing anger or being criticised. Eyebrow raised in anticipation (of rebuke, for example). Expressions change frequently grimace, smile, frown, lowered eyes, within a few seconds	Minimal eye contact. Evasive. Furtive glances. Often looks down or away from the other person. Wrings hands. Hunches shoulders. Steps back. Covers mouth with hand. Nervous movements: shuffles feet, or, if holding anything, fiddles with it. Arms crossed for protection.	Self-blame. Goes round the issue. Avoids the issue. Over-justification. Permission-seeking statements. Gives in easily. Generates sympathy. Makes people feel guilty in order to get what he or she wants.
Aggressive Keen to win, if necessary at the expense of others. Stands up for their rights but also violates the rights of others. Involves expressing needs, wants, opinions, beliefs and feelings in inappropriate ways, often ignoring or dismissing the rights and opinions of others.	Tone cold, may be sarcastic. Hard and sharp. Strident, may be loud. Voice may be raised at end of a sentence. Often the loudest voice.	Fluent and very confident / arrogant. Often abrupt and clipped. Often interrupts, shouts down if interrupted. Stresses blaming words and 'you' words. Often very fast.	Smile may be wry or disbelieving. Scowls when angry. Normal expression is set and unfriendly. Jaw set firm, teeth clenched. Chin thrust forward.	Eyes narrowed and cold. Tries to 'stare you out' and dominate. Looks 'over' you. Challenging posture: fist clenching, thumping, finger pointing. Sits bolt upright or leans forward (invades others personal space). Strides around impatiently. Folds arms unapproachably.	Quick to blame others. Criticises person, not his or her behaviour. Interrupts frequently. Authoritarian. Uses sarcasm, criticism and ridicule to win the point. Makes requests sound like orders. Escalates a situation to confrontation easily.

Behaviour Type	Voice	Speech Pattern	Face	Body Language	Actions
Passive/Aggressive A mixture of behaviour combining passive and aggressive behaviours. Keen to get even without the risk of confrontation.	Sometimes passive and sometimes aggressive tone of voice and can swing between the two.	Mixture of passive and aggressive.	Mixture of passive and aggressive.	Minimal eye contact but looking away rather than down. Tight-lipped, impatient sighs. Exasperated or 'I don't believe it' expression. Closed posture.	Indirect responses. Sarcastic asides. Barbed humour. 'Gets even' indirectly.
Assertive – being genuine, authentic ('for real') and strong This involves standing up for your own rights without violating those of the other person. To do this, you need to express your needs, wants, opinions, beliefs and feelings in a direct, honest, clear and 'adult' way.	Steady and firm. Tone: middle-range, full and warm. Clear Sounds sincere Neither too loud or too soft.	Fluent and confident. Pauses are intentional, not awkward. Key 'action' words are stressed. Even pace. If interrupted, waits, then repeats calmly. Use of 'I' phrases, rather than (accusing) 'you' comments.	Smiles when pleased. Frowns when angry. Normal expression is friendly, approachable and open.	Meets other person's eyes. Does stare them out. Open hand movements, inviting others to speak. Sits upright or relaxed, does not slouch or cower. Stands with head held up. Makes firm and definite movements. Does not fidget.	Lots of listening; seeks to understand. Treats people with respect. Prepared to compromise; solution-focused. Prepared to state and explain what he or she wants. Straight and to the point without being abrupt. Prepared to persist for what he or she wants.

Here are a few examples of how much more effective it is to use assertive language highlighted as **As** rather than Passive P or Aggressive Ag:

As: Please put your dirty washing in the laundry bin. It will only get washed if it's in there.

P: I'm sick of it. You always leave your dirty washing on the floor.

As: (to the person allocating the task) Please help me clarify exactly what you want me to do in this task.

P: I haven't a clue what s/he wants me to do. (to a 3rd person)

As: We obviously have different views on this and think we need to look at the facts and evidence.

Ag: You don't know what you're talking about.

As: Hold that thought. Just let me finish explaining what I mean.

P: (Allowing ourselves to be interrupted).

Ag: Well if you're going to interrupt, we're not going to get anywhere.

The Pros and Cons of the Four Behaviour Types

I'M OK

WIN/LOSE   WIN/WIN

AGGRESSIVE   ASSERTIVE

YOUR'E NOT OK   You're ok

PASSIVE/AGGRESSIVE   PASSIVE

LOSE/LOSE   LOSE/WIN

I'M NOT OK

209

The Benefits of Being Assertive

Assertive behaviour enables us to state clearly our thoughts, feelings and views, and to stand up for our rights whilst treating people with the respect they deserve. It may not guarantee that we achieve what we want, but it does provide three very useful benefits:

- It gives us the best chance of achieving what we want;
- It provides us with the reassurance that we positively played our part in the conversation;
- It helps us to maintain our self-regard and confidence;
- It gives us the best chance of effective relationships and increased capacity to continuously improve in our relationships.

As we interact with others, it's useful to focus on the four essentials of assertiveness:

How people feel about us is largely a direct result of the way we behave towards them; the more positive our behaviour, the more valued we are by our family, friends, work colleagues, tutors, and team mates.

Of course, we are often very forgiving of the way our children, parents and those closest to us behave towards us. We recognise that our children can take out their frustrations on us when they don't feel able to with anyone else. However, that doesn't alter the principle that we have more fulfilling relationships when we behave in a positive, affirming way with each other.)

In summary, assertiveness is the ability to get our views, wants and needs across to others in a calm, rational manner, to stand up for ourselves and say how we feel, when we feel we need to. It includes:

- expressing our own opinions and feelings.
- saying 'No' without feeling guilty.
- setting our own priorities i.e. choosing how we spend our time.
- asking for what we want.

- being able to take reasonable risks.
- choosing not to assert ourselves at times when we feel it would be better to say nothing.

 Teamwork

You can have everything in life you want if you'll just help enough other people to get what they want!
Zig Ziglar

Developing our emotional literacy and assertiveness are essential to work effectively with others, including contributing to, or leading, a team. We may live in an age of high technology, but we also live in an age when the impact of the way we get on together, in work and in life generally, has never been more important. Most of us need to contribute to, and lead, teams: productively co-operate in order to achieve individual, team and organisational goals. Teamwork is a key element of what employers emphasise in any list of what they're looking for in employees, and there is always an emphasis on this in organisational learning and development programmes.

The world-renowned expert on teams in the workplace is Dr Meredith Belbin, author of *Team Roles at Work*, *Management Teams - Why They Succeed or Fail*, and for young people starting out in work, *The Belbin Guide to Succeeding at Work*, amongst many others. I had the privilege to meet him in early 2013 and hear his insights into enabling people to work effectively to achieve shared goals. Dr Belbin maintains that fitness for purpose is crucial if we are to consistently make the most of people's talents and skills in organisations; that is, bringing the most appropriate people together to work on specific tasks and projects rather than confining people in inflexible job roles. I don't intend to go into teamwork in the workplace here, but mention it to reinforce the importance of being able to contribute, lead and manage ourselves effectively within teams, whether that's sports teams or medical teams, or charity teams, our 'domestic' team (at home), or business team.

Elements of Effective Teamwork

Here are a few of the essential elements of effective teamwork. As you read through this list you'll be able to think of ways you, and those around you, use and develop these understandings and skills. You'll also see how they tie in with emotional literacy and being assertive.

Co-operate with others
Fundamental to effective teamwork is co-operation. We don't always like the people we need to work with but a mark of someone who is a good team member and team leader is the ability to work productively with people, as necessary, to succeed in achieving the goal.

Actively listen
Show that we are listening by our body language and ensure we hear what people say, reflect on it, question it, and use it in our thinking.

Ask questions
Ask questions to gain clarification and seek further understanding for ourselves and the team. Avoid passively agreeing.

Encourage others
Use affirming language and body language to encourage contributions. Acknowledge others' skills, experience and potential contribution. Ask for others' views.

> *We cannot hold a torch to light another's path*
> *without brightening our own.*
> Ben Sweetland

Tolerate other people's ideas
There will be disagreements and heated debate in any high-performing team.

Be positive
Positive language and body language create an environment where people are more likely to contribute. A positive, yet challenging,

atmosphere energises people and enables creativity to flow.

Come up with solutions

We all know the '1001 reasons why not' people in teams: those who always produce issues, but no solutions. They drain everyone's energy. Teams need those who come up with ideas and seek solutions: who find ways forward and help others to find ways forward.

Justify opinions

We must expect to justify our opinions and respond to challenge without taking it personally.

Consider other people's views

Listen, hear and reflect on others' views.

Critically evaluate ideas and contributions

All ideas and contributions need to be scrutinised, questioned and evaluated rather than just accepted. This doesn't mean delaying progress by unnecessarily pedantic behaviour. That is simply energy sapping and deflating for a team. Also, don't accept ideas just because of who they come from!

Be willing to change if appropriate

If we listen and are open-minded, we are able to see when changes can achieve better outcomes.

Agree strategies and solutions

Gain agreement and ensure strategies and solutions are actively shared.

Take responsibility

Teams look for team members and team leaders who take responsibility: delivering on their role and helping the team deliver. The 'pass the buck' person is an energy sapper, and soon becomes resented by other members of the team.

Show commitment

Whatever the team task, role or project, team members and team leaders look for commitment from their fellow team members.

Commitment is essential to maintaining focus and drive towards shared goals.

Only the guy who isn't rowing has time to rock the boat.
Jean-Paul Sartre

Organise
Organisation is vital to enable teams to achieve their aims, and those with organisational skills should be valued and listened to just as much as those with technical and creative input.

Decide who will do what
Whether it's a school sports team, a complex work project, or 'Young Enterprise' business team, individuals need to know what their role is and who is doing what if the whole team is to function effectively. If two people are doing the same job, they get in each other's way and, more than likely, another job isn't being done; this applies whether the task is organising a party or implementing a project.

Motivate others
There are times in any team when some members are not at their best, and it's important that members of the team help to motivate each other. Team members need to challenge and support each other to perform at their best to effectively and efficiently achieve goals or win!

Support the team
Team members expect support from each other and from their leaders, just as leaders expect support from their team.

The miracle is this - the more we share, the more we have.
Leonard Nimoy

Trust
To perform at their best, teams need members who trust each other: trust they'll see it through and trust each other to do what they say they're going to do, when they say they're going to do it.

Make it happen

Teamwork is sometimes mistaken for just being nice to each other: getting on well, coming up with creative solutions. They are all aspects, but what the team has to do is deliver the desired outcome! Get it done on time, get it done within budget, win the match etc.

Energy is a recurring theme in the elements of teamwork

Energy givers are crucial to help the team perform at its best, and if all team members are energy givers, the team has an edge. Likewise, energy sappers detract from the team's propensity to perform at its best. Energy-giving behaviour is encouraging, positive, affirming and enthusiastic. Energy-sapping behaviour is detracting, negative, unduly critical and highlights problems without offering solutions. When we watch a sports match, we support one or other team, and it's very usual for teams to say they felt the energy from supporters which boosted their performance.

Successful people relate well with others, develop their emotional literacy and understand the power and value of engaging others. People who achieve personal, social and economic goals are assertive. They feel comfortable in their own skin and gain the respect of those around them. Through constant reflection and a desire to improve, they recognise their strengths and limitations and effectively contribute to, and lead, teams.

Affirmations

- *I am feeling energised from marvellous, mutually beneficial relationships.*
- *I am loving the way we are getting on as a family.*
- *I am always improving my understanding of my feelings and the feelings of those around me.*
- *I am positively contributing to the team and I'm humbled by their trust in me.*

 ACTION

I have developed a number of self-reflection and development tools to help us maintain **C**onstant **A**nd **N**ever-ending **I**mprovement. A few of these are specifically designed to help us reflect on managing relationships.

1. Emotional Literacy

a. Complete the **Emotional Literacy C.A.N.I.**
   Free download on the equipped2succeed website.

b. Think of times when you may not have used your emotional intelligence, and reflect on how you may have acted differently. Think of better alternatives for handling the situations. Share these with another person to gain different perspectives. Another person's view is often affirming.

c. Use the outcomes of activities a and b to identify areas for improvement for yourself and those around you. Further develop your emotional competence, in general, and in specific situations, and practise developing these competencies.

2. Being Assertive

a. Complete the **'How assertive am I?'** questionnaire on the equipped2succeed website, and use the descriptions of assertive, passive and aggressive behaviour to reflect on how you can become more assertive in all situations. It gives us the language and framework to reflect, and enables us to develop more assertive behaviours.

b. Use 'The Four Behaviour Types' summary to help you reflect on your behaviour. Reflect on the extent to which the descriptions apply to you in different situations, and what you can do to be consistently more assertive.
   Highlight the main behaviours you recognise in yourself.

Highlight, from the assertiveness description, the ones you would like to exhibit more often.

c. Using the questions below is another way of reflecting on using more consistently assertive behaviour.
   o List the situations when you are assertive.
     What does being assertive entail in these situations?
     How does it feel?
     What can you do to behave like this more consistently?
   o List the situations in which you behave passively.
     What does being passive look like in these situations?
     How does it feel?
     What can you do to become more assertive in these situations?
   o List the situations in which you behave aggressively.
     What is aggressive behaviour in these situations?
     How does it feel?
     What can you do to become more assertive in these situations?

Become more assertive by going over scenarios with those who you recognise as being well equipped to help you find alternative, more assertive ways of putting things, whether that's asking for something, making a contribution to a discussion, or responding to others.

3. Teamwork

Take every opportunity to work with others, be part of a team, and reflect on how well you contribute and manage relationships with others.
Use the **'Teamwork C.A.N.I'** on the equipped2succeed website to focus on where your strengths are and where you need to improve.

In all this 'people stuff', be prepared to acknowledge and accept your mistakes. Don't beat yourself up about mistakes: apologise, promise yourself and those around you that you will improve in the future, and move on. This is crucial to developing a positive relationship with yourself and others.

> You don't have to be perfect to impress people.
> Let them be impressed by how you
> deal with your imperfections.

What's really important is that we recognise the importance of the 'people stuff' and develop our ability to understand and manage ourselves, working well with people in our many and varied relationships.

> **We must learn to live together as brothers or**
> **we will perish together as fools.**
> Martin Luther King

Chapter Fifteen

Build Resilience

Develop personal capacity to bounce back and persist

build: *make or become stronger or more intense; establish and develop (a business or situation) over a period of time; use as a basis for further development.*

resilience: *able to withstand or recover quickly from difficult conditions.*

persist: *continuing firmly in an opinion or course of action; persisting, especially in spite of difficulty, opposition, obstacles, discouragement; lasting or enduring tenaciously.*

There's only one thing more painful than carrying on and that's giving up!

If one dream should fall and break into a thousand pieces, never be afraid to pick up one of those thousand pieces and begin again.
Flavia Weedn

Being persistent and resilient in the face of adversity is essential if we are to achieve those things that are really important to us. Successful people demonstrate relentless persistence, that 'stickability' and 'never give up' attitude that is essential to do what it takes to attain elite performance in any field of endeavour. There are few better examples of persistence and resilience than two

British athletes who have won seven Olympic gold medals between them, rower Sir Steve Redgrave and athlete Dame Kelly Holmes.

Sir Steve Redgrave won an incredible five gold medals in five successive Olympic Games from 1984 to 2000, as well as a bronze, not allowing diabetes, age or any other obstacle to stop him. Having been diagnosed with diabetes in 1997, he took the same resilient approach to that that he took to any other set-back, '*I decided very early on that diabetes was going to live with me, not me live with diabetes*', and he went on to win his fifth gold medal.

I was privileged to see one of Britain's most successful and celebrated female athletes, Dame Kelly Holmes, win gold gedals in both the 800m and 1500m events at the 2004 Athens Olympic Games. She set British records in numerous events and still holds the records over the 600m, 800m, 1000m, and 1500m distances. Kelly took up athletics in 1982 at the age of 12 and it was a very long journey to her success in Athens. Having entered professional sport quite late, after a successful career in the army, her dedication, drive and never-give-up attitude enabled her to overcome many injuries and set-backs in her career. Her persistence paid off, with numerous records and successes in major competitions, culminating in double Olympic victory at the age of 34.

 There are many words and phrases that can be used to describe the relentless pursuit of getting to where we want to be that these athletes demonstrate:

strength of mind   determination

doggedness   pushiness

willpower   resolve

purpose   grit

hard work (working smart as well as working hard)

Individuals who excel in their field persist: they carry on when the going gets tough, when others give up or don't try quite as hard. In education, business, sport, careers, maintaining a relationship you value, dance, music, earning the money to buy your dream house, in any area of life, persistence is a crucial part of succeeding.

We are determined and persist in the things that are important to us and that we are passionate about. So it's essential to decide what we want, decide what we need to do to get there, decide what we're prepared to pay in time, energy and effort, and persist. If we're passionately working towards something, persistence is an essential ingredient in success. When there are challenges, as there will be, those who are persistent find a way through, round, over, keeping their sights firmly on their goals.

Resilience is the other side of the persistence coin, enabling us to overcome setbacks. It is that inner self-belief and outer protective coating that equip us to persist in pursuing our goals through any manner of hostile environments. That all-important persistence and resilience doesn't happen by accident. It comes from having goals we're passionate about and it comes from believing in ourselves. Most of us need help to develop the sort of persistence that is essential to keep going when the going gets tough, and the resilience to handle difficult times and maintain our self-belief.

> *Patience, persistence and perspiration*
> *make an unbeatable combination for success.*
> Napoleon Hill

Persistence and resilience often means taking what other people view as risks, and having the self-belief to see it through. If you ever feel like giving up on pursuing your goals, just watch the film *The Pursuit of Happyness*. I could have just said watch that film at the start of this chapter and left it at that! It is a 2006 biographical film starring Will Smith, about the, at one time homeless, salesman-turned-stockbroker Chris Gardner.

The film begins in 1981 in San Francisco. Linda and Chris Gardner live in a small apartment with their son, Christopher. Chris has invested the family's life savings in a franchise, selling portable bone density scanners. These scanners provide slightly denser pictures than X-rays, but Chris finds that most of the doctors he visits think they are too expensive. Linda works in a dead-end job in a local hotel laundry. The tension between them mounts as financial pressures increase with unpaid rent and bills continuing to accumulate. Chris often parks his car in 'no parking' areas so he can make scheduled appointments on time, and an accumulation of unpaid parking tickets mean that their car is impounded. After missing a shift at her job, Linda finally leaves with their son Christopher, returns briefly, then departs for a better job in New York City, leaving behind Christopher with his father (at his father's request).

Chris accepts an unpaid internship brokerage firm Dean Witter Reynolds that promises employment to only one trainee. His lack of salary, and his lack of scanners to try to sell, leaves him riddled with debt, and he and his son eventually become homeless. After spending several nights riding buses and sleeping in subway restrooms, saddled with their meagre belongings, they begin lining up at a Church on a daily basis in an effort to secure accommodation for the night. Sometimes they succeed, other times they are literally left out in the cold. As he struggles to provide a semblance of family life for his son under the most difficult of circumstances, Chris becomes more determined to complete the intern program and become the sole trainee the firm will hire.

In the end, Chris gets the job, and in 1987 starts his own brokerage firm, called Gardner Rich. In 2006, he sells a minority of it for a multi-million dollar deal. It's a stark example of relentless pursuit of a goal and the pay-off for persistence. This film should be compulsory viewing for all teenagers, with appropriate discussion afterwards bringing out the learning and how they can apply the lessons in their own lives. The following quotation could easily have been used in this film:

> **Four steps to achievement: plan purposefully, prepare prayerfully, proceed positively, pursue persistently.**
> William Ward

Balancing Challenge and Support:
Review – Review – Review!

We return to the recurring theme of balance. On the one hand, we need people around us who have high expectations and challenge us to continuously improve. On the other hand it's helpful to have that sort of nurturing support we need to help us pick ourselves up when the going gets tough. Sometimes we can find these in the same person and sometimes we need to seek different support from different people. But having the right coaches or mentors around us is always helpful in developing and maintaining our persistence and resilience.

It's also vital that we commit to whatever we take on. Those who 'let others down', in whatever context, soon get a reputation that sticks with them and leads people not to commit to them.

I am not discouraged because every wrong attempt discarded is another step forward.
Thomas Edison

Another important aspect of not giving up when the going gets tough, is creatively finding ways to overcome challenges. This links to Chapter five; *Take Responsibility*, in that we need to take responsibility for finding solutions to challenges, whether that's with appropriate help from others or on our own. This solution-focus and belief in our own capacity to solve problems can be supported through systematic, non-judgemental review, especially when things go wrong. If failure is viewed as a learning opportunity rather than something to be ashamed of, we can to address the things we need to work on in a positive way. The more we find ways through challenges, the more resilient we become: creating that positive, persistent forward momentum we need to achieve our goals.

The sorts of questions we may ask ourselves:
- o What went well?
- o Why do I think that is?
- o What didn't go so well?
- o Why do I think that is?

- o What have I learned?
- o How can I use what I've learned in this and other areas?
- o What can I do to improve?
- o Who can help me with that?

Discipline

Now and then a man stands aside from the crowd, labours earnestly, steadfastly, confidently, and straightway, becomes famous for wisdom, intellect, skill, greatness of some sort. The world wonders, admires, idolizes, and it only illustrates what others may do if they take hold of life with a purpose. The miracle, or the power, that elevates the few, is to be found in their industry, application, and perseverance under the promptings of a brave, determined spirit.
Mark Twain

The discipline of getting the job done, of study, of practice, the discipline of doing whatever we need to do on a daily basis to achieve our goals is a form of persistence that we can learn and turn into a habit. Above all, this requires discipline of thought and, as Dr Steve Peters may say in his brilliant book, *The Chimp Paradox – The Mind Management Programme for Confidence, Success and Happiness*, not allowing our 'Chimp' to take us off track. Discipline means systematically dismissing those thoughts that lead us to deviate from the journey to our goals:

- o *'I can have a day off exercise today. I know I didn't go yesterday but I have ....(whatever we can convince ourselves is more important) ... to do. I'll go for a walk tomorrow.'*
- o *'I'm really not in the right frame of mind to study. I'll just watch this programme first.'*
- o *'I can just have another half hour in bed.'*
- o *'Another day to get that finished won't hurt.'*

Successful people systematically manage their 'Chimp'. They maintain their discipline in the things that are important to them and what contributes to their achievement, no matter what that is. Losing discipline doesn't always mean taking a lazy, line of least resistance route. Personally, I've lost my discipline when I've worked too many hours. I've lost my discipline when I've spent too long with colleagues who needed to talk, which has caused other challenges and time-pressures for me. I should have just arranged a better time. I've lost my discipline on occasions when things have just seemed too tough. It's taken a long time for me to acknowledge it without self-reproach, and use it as an opportunity to refocus my energies and priorities.

Just as intrinsic motivation is much more powerful than extrinsic motivation, being self-disciplined is infinitely more powerful than requiring someone else to prompt or chase us to get things done. Discipline is a habit and therefore practicing it in one context enables us to use it in other contexts. However, just as we can be determined in some things and not in others according to our interests, passions and motivation, we can be disciplined in some things and not in others. It's a matter of aligning our discipline with what matters.

The most valuable learning comes from experience: from success and failure.

Decide what you want, decide what you are
willing to exchange for it.
Establish your priorities and go to work.
H.L. Hunt

Persistence enables us to achieve our potential.
Lack of persistence means we can end up settling for
something less than our dreams.

Affirmations
- *I am persistently pursuing my goals.*
- *I am relishing my achievements one step at a time.*
- *I am feeling energised, breaking down barriers to my success.*
- *I am having fun, reaping the rewards of my persistence.*

- *I am feeling fantastic, working persistently towards my goals.*
- *I am feeling powerful and resilient pursuing my goals.*

* *The Chimp* as defined by Dr Steve Peters: referenced earlier on page 167

Chapter Sixteen

Be the 'Go To' Person

Develop knowledge and skills to be the
best at what you do

I have been impressed with the urgency of doing.
Knowing is not enough; we must apply.
Being willing is not enough; we must do.
Leonardo da Vinci

develop: *to bring out the capabilities or possibilities of;*
bring to a more advanced or effective state;
to cause to grow or expand.

Successful people become experts in their field. They do the work, study and gain experience, to develop their knowledge, understanding, skills and technical ability.

Bill Gates, 'Mr Microsoft', spent thousands of hours learning about computers. When he was in the eighth grade, the Mothers' Club at his school used proceeds from a jumble sale to buy a Teletype Model 33 ASR terminal and a block of computer time on a General Electric (GE) computer for the school's students. Gates took an interest in programming the GE system in BASIC, and was excused from mathematics classes to pursue his interest. He wrote his first computer program on this machine: a version of tic-tac-toe that allowed users to play games against the computer. Gates was fascinated by the computer, and how it would always perfectly execute software code. After the Mothers' Club donation was exhausted, he and other students sought time on other systems. One of these systems belonged to Computer Center Corporation (CCC), which banned four Lakeside students, including Gates, for the summer after it caught them exploiting bugs in the operating system to obtain free computer time. At the end of the ban, the four students offered to find bugs in CCC's software in exchange for computer time, which they did for some years, whilst also writing programmes for other companies and the school's administration. Gates went on to Harvard but did not have a definite study plan and spent a lot of time using the computers, whilst working on various research and commercial activities. Having easily done his '10,000 hours', Bill Gates eventually dropped out of Harvard to start his own company and the rest, as they say, is history.

Much is known of David Beckham and the iconic status he has in the football world. As a youngster, he practised relentlessly, working hard on the things he was good at to become the best. When he was fourteen, he wasn't considered fit enough or strong enough so he worked harder than ever on his fitness and strength, continuously coming top of fitness tests going forward. He was renowned for training harder than anyone whilst at Manchester United, practising free kicks over and over again at the training ground after others had finished, and on school fields near where he lived in 'time off' in the summer.

Mary Kay Ash spent over 25 years working in sales for different companies, firstly part-time as a young married woman to supplement the family income and then full-time. From 1939 to 1962, Mary Kay Ash worked full-time for two different companies and left the second one in 1962 after watching yet another man whom she had trained get promoted over her and earn a much higher salary than her. She started her cosmetics company, Mary Kay Inc., in 1963, aged 45, with her 20 year-old son, using incentive programmes and other strategies to give her employees the chance to benefit from their achievements. The marketing and people skills Mary Kay had learned soon led her company to enormous success. Her goal was to provide women with an unlimited opportunity for personal and financial success. She used her 'Golden Rule' as a guiding philosophy and encouraged employees and sales force members to prioritise their lives according to this simple motto: 'God first, family second, career third'. This was designed to be empowering for women juggling caring responsibilities with work, and was very different to most other company philosophies of the time. Her philosophy was based on years of experience, her deep understanding of sales, the barriers facing women, and the infinite potential of women in the workplace.

Richard Feynman, Nobel Prize-winning physicist, showed, from a very young age, an insatiable curiosity for how things worked, improving things and solving puzzles. He was heavily influenced by his father, who encouraged him to ask questions to challenge orthodox thinking, and who was always ready to listen and teach Richard something new. As a child, he had a passion for engineering, maintained an experimental laboratory in his home, and delighted in repairing radios for people in the neighbourhood and making radios from old discarded ones. Once, he created a home burglary system while his parents were out, activated by someone entering his room. When he started working in a hotel as a teenager, he was always seeking to find better ways of doing things, much to the irritation of the owner and staff when things went wrong. It's great to note that his parents saw working as an essential part of his 'education', especially for someone so academically able, who later became a leading academic of the 20th Century.

At college, Richard did older students' physics assignments to expand his grasp of the subject and relentlessly solved puzzles, informally and formally training his mind for what was to come. He continued to pursue knowledge and broad experience outside his main field of endeavour throughout his life, which informed his physics and contributed to his exceptional achievements.

Marissa Mayer also showed an early interest in maths and science. Whilst at high school, she worked at a local grocery store, where she memorised the prices for hundreds of items in order to streamline the checkout process. Her journey to be President and CEO of Yahoo probably started just after high school when she was selected by the Wisconsin Governor as one of the state's two delegates to attend the National Youth Science Camp in West Virginia. At Stanford University, Mayer developed a passion for computers, and went on to earn both a Bachelor of Science degree in symbolic systems, and a Master of Science degree in computer science, both with a specialisation in artificial intelligence. During her studies, Mayer also taught undergraduate courses in computer programming, earning two teaching awards for her contribution. However, it was her research internships at Stanford University and the Union Bank of Switzerland's research laboratory in Zurich that helped her gain 14 job offers straight out of University, including one from a small company called Google. She joined Google in 1999 as their twentieth employee and was the company's first female engineer. During her thirteen years with the company, she was an engineer, designer, product manager and executive, holding many key roles across the company. She had certainly done a long and detailed 'apprenticeship' by the time she took over at Yahoo.

Sir Richard Branson is one of the most successful entrepreneurs of recent times. He is best known as the founder of the Virgin Group of more than four hundred companies, but he started his business life very young. His first real business venture (after many earlier entrepreneurial activities) was a magazine called *The Student* at the age of sixteen. In 1970, he set up a mail-order record business from the crypt of a church where he ran *The Student*. Branson advertised popular records in the magazine and it was an overnight success. Trading under the name 'Virgin', he sold records for considerably less than the high street stores. Branson once said, *'There is no point in starting your own business unless you do it out of a sense of frustration.'* The name *Virgin* was suggested by one of Branson's early employees because they were all new at business. At the time, many products were sold under restrictive marketing agreements that limited discounting. In effect, Branson began the series of changes that led to large-scale discounting of recorded music.

Oprah Winfrey had a very challenging, now well documented, childhood. However, from a young age, she played games, interviewing her dolls and the crows on the fence when living with her grandmother. Winfrey acknowledges her grandmother's positive influence, saying it was her who had encouraged her to speak in public and 'gave me a positive sense of myself'. As a teenager, she went, for the second time, to live with Vernon Winfrey, whom she viewed as her father. He was encouraging and made her education a priority. Winfrey became an honours student and joined her high school speech team at East Nashville High School, achieving second place in a national 'Dramatic Interpretation' competition. She also won an oratory contest, which secured her a full scholarship to Tennessee State University where she studied communication. Her first job as a teenager was working at a local grocery store. She also worked at a local black radio station in Nashville, which hired her to do the news part-time. She continued to work there during high school and her first two years of college. Working in local media, she was both the youngest news anchor and the first black female news anchor at Nashville's WLAC-TV. Oprah's story reminds me of this quote:

Life is a grindstone.
Whether it grinds us down or polishes us up depends on us.
Thomas L. Holdcroft

Whatever our chosen field of endeavour, if we want to succeed, we need to develop appropriate and specific knowledge, understanding and outstanding technical ability in that field. If we want to achieve elite, out of the ordinary performance, we need to develop elite, out of the ordinary technical ability.

Only a mediocre person is always at his best.
W. Somerset Maugham

 The '10,000 Hours Rule'

The 'Ten Year rule', or '10,000 hours rule', refers to the prolonged, systematic, deliberate practice that is essential to achieve elite performance. It is usually used in a sports context but is relevant in any field of endeavour, whether that's Marissa Mayer's knowledge, understanding and ability to optimise search engines, or Richard Branson's knowledge and insight in business, or Baroness Susan Greenfield's knowledge of the brain, enabling her to write, *The Secret Life of the Brain*.

One of the best books about developing elite performance is Matthew Syed's *Bounce - The Myth of Talent and the Power of Practice*. He uses research, first-hand experience and many examples to demonstrate that elite, world class performance is not about 'talent' but opportunity, environment, hard work, dedication and purposeful, deliberate, high-quality practice. One of the examples he uses is the Polgar sisters.

An extreme example of systematically developing technical ability is the Polgar sisters' experience. Laszlo Polgar advertised for, and found, a wife to collaborate with him to test out his theory that, 'Geniuses are made, not born'. Chess Grandmaster Susan (Zsuzsanna) Polgar and her two younger sisters, Grandmaster Judit and International Master Sofia, were part of their father's educational experiment; he sought to prove that children could make exceptional achievements if trained in a specialist subject from a very early age. He and his wife Klara educated their three daughters at home, with chess as the specialist subject. At age 4, Susan Polgar won her first chess tournament, the Budapest Girls' Under-11 Championship, with a 10–0 score. In 1982, at the age of 12, she won the World Under 16 (Girls) Championship. Despite restrictions on her freedom to play in international tournaments (due to Hungary being within the USSR at that time), by 1984, aged 15, Polgar had become the top-rated female chess player in the world.

In January 1991, Susan Polgar became the first woman to earn the Grandmaster title through tournament play, and she is renowned for breaking a number of gender barriers in chess. In 1992, Polgar won both the Women's World Blitz and the Women's World Rapid Championship. She is the only world champion, male or female, to win all three forms of world chess championships. She is also an Olympic chess champion. Susan is now a chess teacher, coach, writer and promoter and the head of the Susan Polgar Institute for Chess Excellence (SPICE) at Texas Tech University. Her father's experiment of focused, deliberate practice and pursuit of excellence certainly worked in attaining elite performance. It's certainly a similar model to the one followed by Richard Williams and Oracene Price with their daughters, Venus and Serena, and Lewis Hamilton's and Andre Agassi's parents.

As a parent, I have reservations about this as a model for our children's childhood. I have always believed it important to empower, enable and equip our children, as rounded individuals, to pursue their dreams, not mine. However, I also think that only the children involved in such intense programmes have the right to judge. Whatever else, there is no doubt that such examples demonstrate how vital it is to develop the necessary knowledge, technical ability and experience if we want to perform at an elite level in anything.

You must work very hard to become a natural golfer.
Gary Player

 ## C.A.N.I.
Continuous And Never-ending Improvement

Excellence requires a **growth mindset** and a C.A.N.I. approach. Continuous And Never Ending Improvement is an essential part of achieving success in any field.

I Can do Better Philosophy
All successful people are constantly asking themselves – *'How can I do better? How can I improve?'* They practice C.A.N.I.:

Constant
And
Never-ending
Improvement

When you ask yourself, 'How can I do better?', the creative power of your mind is switched on and ways to do things better suggest themselves. When you ask others, experts in your field, 'How can I do better?' they are inevitably willing to help. They are impressed by your attitude, appreciate that you value their experience, and are pleased to be able to help. There are a number ways those who succeed achieve elite performance and continuously improve.

Formal Learning

They progress through educational and training routes in their specialist field, focusing on a specific or niche area, and excelling at each stage. Doing everything they can, they go beyond the normal expectations: further focused, deliberate practice, further research, finding ways to communicate with leaders in their field, internships and other opportunities for specialist work experience, searching out ways to access those special opportunities that set them apart from others in their field.

Informal Learning

Those who succeed and thrive make the most of informal learning opportunities, such as: taking every opportunity to talk to people in the field; traveling to expand their horizons; exploring relevant on-line sources of information and inspiration; reading relevant books and autobiographies of people in their field; watching documentaries and so on. When working with young sports people it always amazes me how few of them have read autobiographies of, or found out about, people who've become elite performers in their sport. What better way to learn than from those who have been there and done it?

Teachers, Mentors, Coaches

Those who succeed are open to improvement, to being taught, coached and mentored. They make the most of learning opportunities, not in a compliant, passive way, but in a discerning way, gaining what they need and what's important for their development. They learn all they can from those with relevant experience and expertise from insightful questioning, intelligent challenge and focusing on what's important to them.

Systematic Reflection

Winners in any field, those who achieve the pinnacle in their profession, out-perform others in business and win in sports systematically reflect all the time. They review every step of the way to ensure they are on track. Winners constantly de-brief: every step, every event, every milestone, success and failure:

    A. What did I want to happen?
    B. What actually happened?
    C. What caused the gap?
    D. What am I going to do about it?

Winners expect and positively use feedback. They want those whose opinion they value to critically appraise their performance. They accept or question advice for further understanding and act on it as appropriate.

Winners strive to be at their best

Whatever the field, on a potential scale, if potential is ten, winners consistently achieve ten and constantly seek to go beyond ten. They appreciate that there are no short cuts to As becoming A+s and they seek to maximise their potential at any given moment. Whether their A is in education, a career, business, sport, engineering, arts or academic research, leaders in any field are always trying to convert their As into A+s.

> *Every success is built on the ability to*
> *do better than good enough.*
> unknown

 Marginal Gains

The concept of Marginal Gains is very much associated with Dave Brailsford, who became Performance Director of British Cycling in 1996. He has developed and led a culture of constant improvement and increasingly remarkable performances during that time. He spoke openly about the simple concept of marginal gains when interviewed on BBC Breakfast during the London 2012 Olympics.

'The whole principle came from the idea that if you broke down everything you could think of that goes into riding a bike, and then improved it by 1%, you will get a significant increase when you put them all together,' he explained.

'There's fitness and conditioning, of course, but there are other things that might seem on the periphery, like sleeping in the right position, having the same pillow when you are away and training in different places.'

'Do you really know how to clean your hands? Without leaving the bits between your fingers? If you do things like that properly, you will get ill a little bit less.' (NB: As athletes train at such high intensity, their immune system can often be suppressed which makes them prone to illness.)

'They are tiny things but if you clump them together it makes a big difference.'

This exemplifies how important it is to look at every aspect of how to improve.

Britain won two bronze cycling medals at the Atlanta Olympics in 1996. They won seven out of ten track cycling gold medals in London 2012, matching their achievement from Beijing 2008.

What could you do to make marginal gains in your life?
What could you do to make marginal gains in your
quest to realise your goals?

Take and Make the Most of Opportunities

Successful people spot, take and make the most of opportunities. Opportunities to learn, work, pursue their passions, seek out the right contacts and talk to people who can help them, take onboard coaching and demonstrate the sort of work ethic that 'goes the extra mile'. They are the ones who study that bit longer, are first there at training and last to leave, take that internship hundreds or thousands of miles from home, and make the most of it. They are the first to set their stall up on the market or keep their shop open later than everyone else.

Box of Tools

Many people who attain elite performance or become leaders in their field talk about their tool-kit, or box of tools, that has helped them to develop and maintain excellence. This book is about developing your generic tool-kit, but there are things we need to do that are specific to developing our technical ability in our chosen field of endeavour. The contents of our box will be many and varied, with unique elements that we, as individuals, need. Successful people learn, adopt and adapt tools from many and varied sources; their tool-kit goes beyond the norm. These tool-kits include all of the elements mentioned above, tailored specifically for their needs, relevant to their field and them as an individual. Whatever we pursue, it's vital that we find out what we need in our specific tool-kit and do everything we can to develop the excellence essential for success.

The foundation of lasting self-confidence and self-esteem is excellence, mastery of your work.
Brian Tracy

 Financial Capability (or Financial Literacy)

One of the essential technical competencies is financial capability. It doesn't matter what interest or what endeavour we pursue, we all need to be financially competent. I like the phrase financial literacy because it is a concept we can easily understand. We can all relate to the importance of essential basic literacy. My financial mistakes over the years have reinforced the importance of this for me.

The first stage of this is learning the importance of economic self-determination and the basics of money management. This includes the ability to manage personal finances effectively and become questioning and informed consumers of financial services. Financial literacy can be divided into three interrelated themes:

Knowledge and Understanding: familiarity with a range of concepts such as credit and investment and banking basics;

Skills and Competence: budgeting, financial planning and personal risk management;

Attitudes – thinking through, and taking responsibility for, the wider impact and implications of money and our financial decisions, which includes the following topics:

- o saving for the things you want;
- o understanding your attitude to money: risk and reward;
- o deciding whether something is a want or a need;
- o prioritising saving and spending;
- o being economically independent.

For me, this also includes making informed decisions about investing in your own knowledge, understanding and skills through formal and informal education and learning.

In conclusion, I think the following quote, from one of the all-time greats of golf, succinctly sums up that disciplined, hard work and development of our knowledge and skills is essential to attain elite performance in our chosen fields.

The harder I work the luckier I get.
Gary Player

 ACTION

Do your research in your passion / chosen field of endeavour:

Explore relevant on-line sources of the latest experience and research in your field;

Read books by people who have achieved success in that field;

Find out what examination grades are required in your field.

Find out whatever statistics / records there are that apply to elite performance in your field.

Find people nearby who can help you; who can act as a coach or mentor.

How Can I do Better Today?

Each day, before you begin to do anything, devote 10 minutes to thinking 'How can I do better today?' Ask yourself:
How can I encourage my friends, family, work colleagues, people I lead, class-mates?
What special favour can I do for my friends?
How can I increase my personal efficiency – how can I get things done better and quicker?
How can I do something positive to take another step forward towards my goals?

Do the work, day-by-day, to improve your knowledge, skills, experience, and technical ability in your chosen field to achieve elite performance and become the 'go to' person.

Do your work with your whole heart,
and you will succeed; there's so little competition.
Elbert Hubbard

Have the Life You Deserve
and
Make the Most of the Journey

I sincerely hope that this book is a small contribution towards enabling you to make the most of opportunities and realise your goals.

In the introduction, I said that I wanted the book to be affirming, and I truly hope that it'd helped you to celebrate your strengths and recognise the value of your journey so far. Recognising where you are, what you've learned along the way, and your capacity to create your own positive future.

The equipped2succeed framework is, in itself, a tool for continuous reflection and improvement. Simultaneously holistic and compartmentalised, we are all better at some elements than others at different times. The important thing is that we are always learning, improving and growing.

There are obviously many ways equipped2succeed can be used by individuals, and with different people in different contexts, but I have no doubt that the importance of developing these capabilities has never been greater. I truly appreciate you taking time to read this book and, if we haven't done so already, it would be great to connect, via the equipped2succeed website, on twitter @beverleyburton or on LinkdedIn at Beverley Burton.

> *Life isn't about finding yourself.*
> *It's about creating yourself.*
> George Bernard Shaw

Acknowledgements

I would like to express my immense gratitude to all those people who have helped me develop the work shared in this book: those who have supported my relentless desire to enable people to improve their capabilities to succeed and thrive; those who have tolerated my enthusiasm and those who have been there for me.

Professionals from many fields have informed the concepts in this book. I would also like to acknowledge my debt of gratitude to all those who have shared their life and work; from whom I have learned and continue to learn. A full bibliography is on the equipped2succeed website.

However, I have learned most from the people with whom I've worked: young people, directors, sports people, carers, educators, those who are reaching the pinnacle of professional success, those who are succeeding in their second chance journey and those who have developed wellbeing in all areas of their life. Their willingness to engage with the concepts, critical self-reflection, challenge and feedback has helped me to find the best ways to unlock the amazing potential and brilliance we all have.

Per-Olof Lindroth in Sweden, Dag Ofstad in Norway, Elizabetta Delle Donna in Italy, and Anca Colibaba in Romania have enabled me to embed self-development into European training programmes. Errol Lawson has been unerringly supportive: helping me to deliver these concepts in passionate, insightful ways. Gary Brazil's belief in the value of my work enabled me to work with young footballers, coaches and parents, at a time in football when mindset and mental health were rarely integrated into young players' programmes. Paul Davies has been invaluable in developing work for the benefit of local communities in the UK. I am humbled and honoured by their trust and grateful for their unstinting support and honest feedback.

Thank you to Full Phat for the equipped2succeed designs, always patient with me in translating my ideas into graphics. A special thank you to Christine Redding, for bringing her brilliance to proof reading this book, and offering honest, invaluable advice.

35995476R00137

Printed in Poland
by Amazon Fulfillment
Poland Sp. z o.o., Wrocław